Who put the 'fun' in funeral?

Diary of a Funeral Director

Jan Tury

authorHOUSE®

AuthorHouse™ UK Ltd.
500 Avebury Boulevard
Central Milton Keynes, MK9 2BE
www.authorhouse.co.uk
Phone: 08001974150

©2011 Jan Tury. All rights reserved.

No part of this book may be reproduced, stored in
a retrieval system, or transmitted by any means
without the written permission of the author.

First published by AuthorHouse 05/16/2011

ISBN: 978-1-4567-7618-3 (sc)

Any people depicted in stock imagery provided by Thinkstock are models,
and such images are being used for illustrative purposes only.
Certain stock imagery © Thinkstock.

This book is printed on acid-free paper.

Because of the dynamic nature of the Internet, any web addresses or
links contained in this book may have changed since publication and
may no longer be valid. The views expressed in this work are solely those
of the author and do not necessarily reflect the views of the publisher,
and the publisher hereby disclaims any responsibility for them.

Definition

undertaker

A person whose profession is the preparation of the dead for burial or cremation and the management of funerals; funeral director

Dedication

To Dan, Jord and Heidi. Three great kids that I am exceptionally proud to call my children.

I trust each of them that one day they will find me a bloody good nursing home.

Acknowledgements

Along the way I have met some really great people, and without them, I would not have had a story to tell.

In writing this, it is in memory of those unforgettable characters that have made my life so special.

In the face of adversity, there has always been someone there when I least expected, to give me a push in the right direction again. Good fortune would have it that I have met the right people at the right time and I will be eternally grateful for those that have supported me both emotionally and psychologically in the pitfalls of life. As I have got older the family and friends have become fewer, but they are people I choose to be around and that is just fine with me. If there is one thing I have learnt while spending most of my life in this profession, is that no matter what happens along the way, Life is there to be lived; it doesn't last forever so don't waste it on trivial things and embrace it with every opportunity like it was the last.

Contents

Dedication	v
Acknowledgements	vii
Foreword	xi
1. The Inspiration	1
2. First Day	7
3. Introductions	11
4. The Ropes	16
5. Back Home	19
6. Back for more	22
7. School for the last time	31
8. My new 9-5 job	35
9. The Ultimatum	40
10. My First Real Test	45
11. Ship of the desert	49
12. Dust to Dust	52
13. Summer in Winter	54
14. Slow, Slow, Quick Quick Slow	57
15. Sabbatical	61
16. A Question of Faith	66
17. And now for something completely different	74
18. A very public affair	79
19. I felt like the exercise anyway	84
20. Just making a point	88
21. Trust me	92
22. That's just grate	96
23. Themes	99
24. Time please	103
25. Hey big spender	107
26. Harmonising	111
27. Full moon	115

28. Highly Infectious	119
29. Ding Ding	124
30. A change is as good as a rest.	127
31. Independent	130
32. Ashes to ashes	134
33. Dad moves to Hungary	137
34. A new start	140
35. Accents	147
36. The Big Taboo	152
37. Awareness	157
38. A question of taste	161
39. Changing opinions	165
40. Non Religious	171
41. Exhaustion	176
42. Grinding Halt	180
43. Arrangements	184
44. R's	187
45. Conclusion	189

Foreword

I had intended to write this years ago when my mind was sharper and the memories clearer, but raising a family takes care of any spare time you might have been afforded for such luxuries. I am a self confessed workaholic and have always pushed my physical and mental limits to the full. Of all the goals I have set myself, writing this has been one of the most challenging. In doing so, I have been able to confront certain issues I had for so long buried, and finally lay them to rest.

My philosophy has always been that you don't get anything in life for free. If you want something you must go out and get it, rarely save birthright does anything land on your lap and the path you carve requires a little bit of effort on your part. I believe that at least once in a lifetime we all have a chance to change our destiny; it may not always be obvious and you can guarantee it will come at a time when you least expect it.

I would be a fool to say that taking the leap of faith was the hard part because it isn't. I hope in writing this, it will highlight the peaks and troughs of what I am proud to call *'my profession'* and give the reader an unbiased account of whether it was all worth it.

We have but one short life to do as we see fit and we all have the mind to choose how we lead it. It would be fair to say that I wasn't ready for any major upheaval in my life when it happened to me, but believe me those opportunities don't come knocking every day; you can choose to let it go and always be left wondering *'If only'* or you can take my lead and grab the bull by the horns and just go for it.

If when the time comes I have been lucky enough to fulfil everything I had hoped to do then I will have no qualms and will gladly lay down my top hat and cane.

One word of advice – Buckle up and hold on tight and prepare yourself for one hell of a ride.

Caveat Emptor – Let the buyer beware!

1. The Inspiration

I wanna be a Spaceman, well not really, but for those of you who can remember when you were young enough to think what you might be when you grew up, what else could you have said. I can remember the primary school teacher would often ask this question, and at the time space travel was big – I was four or five when the news broke about Neil Armstrong being the first man on the moon.

I also remember nearly every lad my age wanting to be a train driver (Casey Jones was very popular on TV at that time also).

Of course every lad my age wanted to be a Footballer or a Rock Star, neither of these at the time massively overpaid like they are today and certainly not a job for life.

The expectation of my upbringing in the small rural village of Witcombe where I grew up was that you left school as soon as and followed in the footsteps of one of your family.

For me this meant Farming, Factory or Lorry Driving. Alas none of the above ticked any boxes for me, although I had liked the idea of Truck driving if only for the approval and recognition from my Dad that I would one day be someone he could be proud of.

Funny how life turns out really, although having dabbled very faintly with Farming, Factory work and shunting wagons in a Timber yard in later years, nothing could have prepared me for the calling that brought me to the Profession I have spent in and around the last 30 years or so.

I don't think any kid ever really considers being an Undertaker when he or she grows up, and I was no exception. Work was for grownups and I had plenty of time before making any life changing decisions like that, or so I thought.

Over the years, many many people have asked what made you come into this. Was it a Family Business? etc. etc.

The defining answer to this is I simply don't know, and no it wasn't a Family Business. All I can say is that in 1980 it was the norm that the Careers Officer at school would find placements for all the last year students to spend a week with a recommended employer – unpaid of course, to gain some experience of what the big wide world was all about.

I was brought up in a working class environment and back then if you didn't work there was no money, not like the benefits system we have in place today where you could possibly be better off by not working at all, and so it was that if you had a job you hung on to it. I had a lot of respect for all those around me who took great pride in the jobs they did for a living even if what they did was something I could never see myself doing.

Of course education is important, but so is working for a living, and generally the latter was far more important to working families like mine. There was always plenty of communication within my family, after all we, that is to say Grandparents, Aunties, Uncles, and Cousins all lived in this same little village and everyone knew everybody's business. This was village life and yet I always struggled with the lack of privacy of not knowing who might walk through the door unannounced next.

I wasn't brought up with any special privileges and life was very strict and hard (they used to call this character building). To be honest, if I could have skipped the first 16 years of my life, I would have; and if you had asked me the same question now I would still say the same. I didn't like my childhood, there wasn't much about it to like, which is why I guess I knew if I wanted things to change, I would have to find my own way. I had quite clear ideas on what I didn't want to be when I left school - No I wasn't going to work in a factory, No I wasn't going to be a Farmer and by now I had even gone off the idea of being a Truck Driver.

So, the day came when the Careers Officer had before him the compiled list of recognised employers for the 191 students to choose where they would like to go for the week. I knew there would be nothing for me; I just couldn't imagine doing what everyone else did even if it was a week off school. All said and done, nothing had prepared me for the flash of inspiration that sprung from nowhere while I contemplated my uncertain future as I made my way to the Career Officers room. One by one like lambs to a slaughter we took it in turn to receive our fate. As I entered and made myself comfortable the Careers Officer asked if I had any thoughts where I might like to spend the week, half expecting me to pick one of the above from a generated list of employers that had been given me.

I reflected on the moment as I chewed my bottom lip and not knowing how my response might be received, I looked up, took a deep breath and said that 'I...would like to be ...an ...Undertaker!' If he had read my school report I am sure he would have felt he was being sent up. Luckily he didn't.

'Ah' he said *'We don't have one of those'*. So that was the end of that – not quite. Please don't ask where this inspiration came from, as I simply don't know; somehow though it just felt right even if it did come across as being somewhat rebellious not conforming to *'the norm'*. Whatever the job was supposed to be, it didn't matter – it was different – I was different. Finally, something in my life started to click, and it was dare I say almost exciting as the big wide world lay beckoning.

I had now made my first important decision in life, and without any hesitation popped into the local Undertakers where I met the Funeral Director who was only a few years older than me. He was very pleasant and chatty, nothing like I thought he might be and said he was the youngest qualified Funeral Director in the Country. I took a lot of encouragement from this and after my first insight from stepping foot inside an Undertakers knew that this was something worth looking at. He did however apologise that they would not be able to accommodate such a request, but that he would give a friend of his a call from one of the larger companies in town. I don't know what was said, save to say that not too long after, I did get a call from the Manager of the company who in turn told me to give him the details of my Careers Officer at school and would see what they could do.

On my return to school the next week, I was called into the Careers Office, again resigned to the possibilities of placements where I might be sent. Mr Chapple had been the Careers Officer for the school since the inception of work experiences and was well suited to the position for his businesslike approach. I could see by his expression as he looked over his half frame glasses at me that even he was amused at my designated placement, *'Well, this is a first, we have never had a placement in a Funeral Directors before'.*

Mr Chapple didn't normally interact with pupils as everything he did was all pretty much matter of fact and didn't feel the need to waste good time on small talk. His face wore a Monday morning look every day of the week, and yet for the first time, a glint and dare I say a smile broke rank from his usual guarded guise. On this note he shook my hand and wished me luck. He wasn't wrong there, but it wasn't just the job that I had to consider, I had to break the news to my Mum and Dad what I had done. I guessed, no probably hoped that Mum would be okay with this, after all it was only one week, and sure enough she was. Dad however was not impressed and to say he hit the roof was an understatement. Dad's word was the final word on everything and woe betides anyone that challenged it. What he said stuck. There was no bend in Dad, no compromise, no nothing – he was the law in his own house and made sure everyone knew it.

Things went downhill very quickly from here which I had kind of anticipated anyway, but I wasn't about to just concede even if I was fearful of the repercussions. I had spent a whole lifetime doing just that, and now it was time to make a stand for something I wanted to do. For the most part, everyone else in the family was okay, not overjoyed, but okay. It goes without saying that from the outset you will need to have a very thick skin as you will be in the line of fire for all the one liners ever thought up about funeral parlours, like *'It's a dead end job'* or *'you'll need a stiff upper lip for that'* to name but a couple. I can hear you groan already – you should try listening to it hundred times over!

It would be fair to say that people generally cannot get their heads around why anyone could possibly want to do this for a living and that there might be something wrong with you. One day you're just the same as everyone else and the next you have apparently grown two heads. For Dad, well, I kept out of his way as much as I could for the time he was at home. Fortunately Dad spent most of the week away Lorry driving around the Country, but when he was at home, it was just better to be somewhere else. There were plenty of times I wanted to reason with Dad but I always retreated from that foolish idea as quick as I contemplated it for the fear of being reminded I wasn't too big for a good hiding. I knew I had disappointed Dad, as I wasn't going to be what he had hoped for. I had spent a whole childhood waiting for an approval and acceptance of who I was but sadly that never came, so I guess we can call that stalemate.

2. First Day

How can anyone ever forget their first day at work – not many I bet? This wasn't your normal 9-5 job though, and as I had found out throughout my working life in the business, there are quiet times and there are busy times, even the large conglomerates couldn't truthfully say they are busy busy all the time, even if they would have you believe that. Don't get me wrong, when it is busy you know about it, and you can throw away any ideas of any breaks through the day, but then there are the quiet times when you have completely run out of things to do, I mean how many times can you wash a car or polish a brass candlestick? Sadly there are too few times when there is a steady flow; that would be far too easy, and I guess in a way that's what makes this the best job in the world and also the worst job in the world.

Psychologically speaking, as long as you have an open mind and not too easily offended, then it is a job for life. All said, it is damn near impossible to get a job in the funeral profession in the first place – nobody ever leaves (dead man's boots they call it). It turns up once in a blue moon, so for me I realised just how privileged I was albeit for a week to enter this almost secretive society shrouded in mystical taboos. For me it was like being enrolled for MI5. It was made very clear from the start that you don't talk about the behind scenes activities to anyone outside of work. Wow I thought, this really wasn't your normal 9-5 job. I was excited and nervous at the same time. I had no insight to the funeral world nor experience or even what the role entailed. My pre conceived ideas worked overtime, much of which wasn't anything like what really goes on behind the scenes, but that's another story.

My story begins, and is in dedication to some really fine colleagues many of whom have since passed away. Without those that took me under their wing, I wouldn't have a story to tell.

I remember walking towards the funeral parlour that first morning, and as I did, with every step closer to the office my legs became somewhat heavy laden and almost cemented to the path. Who was I kidding; okay I have proved my point, I had got the placement, the first of its kind for any work experience from school. I had stubbornly stood my ground and put up with the unpleasantries at home, so maybe this is where I can say I proved a point! To be honest, I tried to find any excuse to turn around and go back home, but then I balanced up all that I had gone through to get here. The ridicule would have been far worse, and I could just see my Dad saying *'I told you so'*. For this reason alone I took a deep breath opened the office door and went in.

I was greeted by a very kind lady who asked of my business, to which I had said I was there for a week's work experience. *'You'll have to wait for Mr Compton, he won't be long'* and so I did.

Now remember this is only 1980, but this was before health and safety or any of the dos and don'ts of today. To be honest, my lasting impression of that first encounter was the unbreathable fathoms of nicotine smoke as I walked in. This was quite a normal way of life in most businesses back then. I must admit though, it was probably the last place I would have expected it.

I didn't notice Mr Compton coming in, perhaps he was already there, just not ready to see me until 9.00 a.m. sharp. Mrs Wadley approached me and said that Mr Compton was now ready to see me and pointed me to an upstairs office. The staircase was the same as the front office with a mouldy sort of smell that had an obvious damp proofing problem. Across the landing in front of me was this very dark oak panelled door and a sign that read 'Managers Office'. I tapped on the door almost mouse like trying to envisage who might be behind it. Funny looking back that I imagined someone like Bela Lugosi falling out of the rafters - trust me the imagination is a powerful thing when it plays tricks on you. There was no reply, and rather than tap pathetically again, I nervously entered the inner sanctum of where the day to day organising of funeral activities ran, not really knowing what to expect next. You know even looking back now; it was really funny as I wondered if indeed I would even see my family again. Those moments on reflection are priceless and it wasn't even 9.15a.m.

Before me again was a hovering billow of smoke which seemed to roll around the room like a tidal fog on a riverbank but with the obvious smell of nicotine. The morning sun shone through the upstairs window which beamed horizontally toward me, leaving me with no more an image than a silhouette of Mr Compton sat behind a directors desk with an accompanying ashtray and fag to hand.

'Sit down' he said as he beckoned me forward. Really I don't remember much of what had been said in the few moments I was there, I was too nervous, and my answers were probably quite pathetically lame. Mr Compton was a man of very few words whom I will never forget. He reminded me of someone that could have passed for being a Sicilian Godfather with gravelly voice to match albeit with a West Country Gloucestershire accent. He even dressed similarly with a broad band pinstripe suit in chocolate brown. I had wondered if this may have been at some time originally black in colour but for the nicotine cloud that had impregnated the fabric. Oddly enough, I imagined him to be a tall 6 foot plus man, but in reality was not much taller than 5'2, quite portly and walrus like. Every movement, every word was unrushed but deliberate. Mr Compton was a good man, and he put the wheels in motion for what was a very enlightening first week at work in the big wide world.

3. Introductions

Well, I had survived the initiation - I think, and went back down the staircase a lot quicker than I had gone up. Mrs Wadley took it upon herself to do the introductions. If ever there was a person to make you feel at ease and yet at the same time intimidated it was her. She was almost a welcoming committee all of her own. *'I'm Mrs Wadley, but you can call me Sheila'*. I felt uncomfortable with first names as I had always thought it disrespectful to call someone very senior to me by their Christian name, particularly if you didn't know them. Mrs Wadley was it would be fair to say a life and soul type of person, never a dull moment with her around, very playful but never expected to be anything but one of the lads. *'Don't worry my dear, I'll look after you'*. I wasn't sure whether this was supposed to comfort me or for me to run a mile as it sounded more like an innuendo than a well meant offer of support.

This was Mrs Wadley all over though, and she was like it with everyone, and so I grew to like and respect her, even if she did at times make me burn up the brightest colour of red through embarrassment. She took full advantage of the fact I was only 16 and a very naive 16 at that. It was all well meant fun though, for me and for everyone else as well, as I was teased constantly throughout that first week by her over friendly ways.

As in Mr Compton's office, the downstairs office also doubled as the arranging room and was always full of the smell of smoke; goodness knows what people coming in to arrange funerals thought of this. Mrs Wadley spoke in a way that replicated the same gravelly voice as Mr Compton as she puffed and chatted, tapping away the spent ash into the tray that sat prominently as if part of the stationary on the reception desk. Now if I had thought, Undertakers were stiff upper lipped people, then I think for the most part that preconceived idea went straight out of the window there and then. Mrs Wadley reminded me of one of those mischievous playful characters from a Carry On film that dropped innuendos into most conversations. The same couldn't be said for the assistant manager Mr Donald Reeves who was your very stereotyped undertaker. He just glanced up totally disinterested, gave a grunt and carried on busying himself with his paperwork. Donald Reeves was pencil thin, anaemic and probably in need of a good meal, his bloodshot eyeballs protruded out of their sockets and looked sadder than a grieving bloodhound. The redness on the inner eyelid was as if pencilled on with a thick point bingo marker. You couldn't keep eye contact with him too long in conversation as you would feel your own eyes starting to bleed. Donald Reeves was the 2IC to Mr Compton and he was always deadly serious about something or other even when the mood was light and airy. I guess he felt that as the natural successor to Mr Compton one day, he had to play his part. Goodness knows what made him tick but he seemed genuinely happy with himself even if he did try to carry the whole of the world's problems on his shoulders.

'This is Roy' Mrs Wadley said *'and he will keep you under his wing for the week. Anything you need to know, just ask him'*. Greetings aside, I started to now feel the anxiety loosen. Roy too, was very pleasant and said that he would take me up to the 'Coffin Shop' soon. *'You mean there is a Coffin Shop?'* I exclaimed somewhat surprised realising how daft that must have sounded once I had said it. *'You'll see'* he said. *'There you'll meet the rest of the lads, two of which have started this week as well'*.

I was somewhat relieved to jump in the car with Roy just to get out of the office that was by now testing my oxygen levels in my chest, something over time that I would get used to.

We took the short ¼ mile drive to the industrial estate where the companies others departments were as well. Through the gatehouse and barrier to the estate were the garages, the spray shop, the recycling shed, the admin to the stores, the works canteen and yes, the Coffin Shop. The Coffin Shop was where all the manual work was done. It was where the coffins were held in racks awaiting disposal.

As Roy opened the door to the coffin shop, all of a sudden the mood became more relaxed, okay the familiar cloud of smoke was prominent again but I was now among what would become my equals. The kettle was on as it invariable always was. *'One thing to learn very quickly about this job Jan, is grab a cuppa whenever you can, you never know when the next one will be'*. This was more than just a subtle hint that I would be expected to be the new tea boy. I had never drunk a cup of tea in my life, let alone made one – did they really know what they were letting themselves in for? Roy was of normal build and had what could only be described as a very fine beard (almost like baby hair) and spoke quite effeminate. Roy was always hands on and never needed asking twice to get on with a job. I never quite worked out though how Roy somehow always managed to take two steps to everyone else's one, his legs obviously so much shorter than average and because of his double pace it always felt as if he was in a rush. All said, Roy was a good worker and kept me under his wing for that first week teaching me whatever he could whenever he could. In a way I think he enjoyed this role as I got the impression he didn't keep many friends, and as I was unknowing and unbiased to all, made for a good tutor/pupil relationship even if it was just for five days.

Roy introduced me to the three likely lads who were already slumped into the worn out settees, tea and fags in hand.

Colin was the rebel, the non conformist. He had been with the company some time and was Roy's equal. The difference being, Colin would find every opportunity to get out of doing any work at all. He was for all his faults a lovable rogue, and despite his lazy and lethargic ways, you couldn't help but like him, frustrating that he was at times, could always make you smile as he had a catalogue of one line jokes he used to come out with everyday.

Unfortunately Colin always sailed too close to the wind, and probably had enough written warnings to wallpaper the staffroom twice over. Mr Compton however, was more than a fair man, and despite many calls to get rid of him by other members of staff, always gave Colin a second chance, then a third and fourth etc. Inconsistently with everyone else's dress code Colin was usually untidy. His shirts had more creases than the lines on the palms of your hands, trousers usually had a stain of some sort or another on them and jacket so badly fitted it may as well have come from the local Charity Shop. Although very English, Colin had an afro that was as out of control as a roadside bramble. He was gangly and moved awkwardly almost as if his legs were made of rubber. Colin had already briefed the two new chaps Tony and Reg, which was probably not the best idea in the world as they no doubt would have been given the lowdown on how to do as little as possible in as long a time that could be dragged out meaning someone else would ultimately do what you should have done 8 hours before. Colin was a practical joker, and I think this was the precedent for what Tony and Reg felt was to be their roles in time. I don't think they needed too much persuasion there though!

Tony and Reg were like Laurel and Hardy, (not in features) but in their constant battle to outdo the other. This was to be the case for the next ten years or so. Secretly, I know they couldn't work without each other, even if they did constantly run each other down. For what it's worth, they may as well have been married to each other.

Over the years, Tony and Reg became good friends of mine. We had the same common denominator just as you would at school when you start on the same day; a relationship and bond that remains with you forever. I was always 'piggy in the middle' though as I would usually be the mediator if they had fallen out by passing messages backwards and forwards. They could be like the two grumpy old men on the park bench at times, but when one was off on holiday you knew the other wasn't happy until they came back. They could be both as stubborn as mules when they wanted to be, but whenever one had very real problems the other was always there to support.

4. The Ropes

Naturally, my mind was on information overload, and I wanted to impress. I listened and hung on every word Roy told me. Roy took me through to the coffin store. The small archway from the coffin shop to the coffin store can only be described like walking through to some underground catacomb. The floor was uneven, the room dark and cold, and the limited view I had as my eyes were still adjusting from light to dark was of wooden racking all around. As Roy flicked the switch on, an avenue of overhead lights came on one at a time exposing the storeroom of its contents. I was amazed to see so many coffins all individually rested on racks up to 4 tiers high around the sides of the walls.

The coffins were all sizes, designs and veneers, some solid timbers too. There was me thinking, there was only one type. Roy enthusiastically started to reel off the names of the different types of coffins assuming I was going to be able absorb all this in one go. I acknowledged politely and nodded my head in the right places as if to share the same enthusiasm. He was as mindful about all the names of the coffins as my cousin was with all the names of his 200+ herd of cows. When people are this passionate about their jobs, I begin to wonder if it's a passion or an obsession, the latter probably not being too healthy. Roy, thankfully wasn't the latter, just a workaholic.

Roy had a list of coffins to prepare for the day which he pulled from his top pocket. The coffins are delivered in bulk a hundred at a time by Lorries from the main supplier and are only shells, that is to say veneered top, bottom, sides and ends. It was part of the job to furnish the coffin with handles on the outside and line the inside so as to be waterproof and finish off with a nice satin frill to complete. An engraved nameplate was then placed on the top with the deceased name, date of death and age for identification purposes. I was very practical growing up always making things like go karts and sledges from planks of wood and a hammer and nails and so undaunted by this I was quite excited about putting my skills to good use. Little did I know then, that I would spend the majority of that week doing just that. In truth, it was one of those jobs, that although being essential, was always left to the junior to do, as the rest of the gang always seemed to justify their absence by doing something else far more pressing, co incidentally always arriving back in time for the last coffin being made up, and a welcome cuppa too. I wondered if there was some kind of surveillance camera letting them know when to come back.

Roy was able to fully furnish a coffin in around ¾ hour and did so with no effort or thought as this was something he had done so many times before and probably could have done it blindfolded. Colin on the other hand would always take twice the time and more often than not never finish what he started only for Roy to complete later.

Now if there is one thing I hate, it is someone looking over your shoulder while you're doing something. This was a learning process however, and I had to show willing, so it was a grin and bear it time until I had shown I could master each task confidently on my own. All said, Roy was a good teacher and supportive with everything I tried. Roy also showed me how to operate the engraving machine which was huge and made of a cast iron frame, much taller than me. The settings were complex and there was an element of skill to use it safely and competently unlike today where an engraving machine is very easy to operate and can sit unassuming on the corner of a desk top no bigger than the size of a printer. Another task learnt. I was starting to enjoy this. It was nothing like school and certainly nothing like I expected the first day to go in an undertakers. A short walk across the yard from the coffin shop was the works canteen. It was always a welcome break when you had the chance to pop in for a warm up and change of scenery. The cafe menu was hardly of Michelin standard but good honest British food which usually consisted of chips with everything. It was also a good social place to go where people from all departments mixed. Managers and staff alike were equals here albeit for the ½ hour break.

As the end of the day approached I felt as if I had done two days in one. The excitement of getting through the day in one piece left my head spinning and I looked forward to going home to share all what I had done. Roy said as we walked out of the estate passed the gatehouse that that was where I would need to clock in the next morning. On this we said our goodbyes and went our separate ways.

5. Back Home

The bus journey back seemed to take forever to get me to my stop, and then it was a still another ½ mile walk back to Mum and Dad's. As tired as I was from the first day I was buzzing with excitement and kept thinking of the things I would tell everyone. I couldn't wait to share what I had learnt and the people I had met. As I walked the last stretch home I wondered what kind of reception I would get assuming everyone else in the family bar one would be eager to find out how I fared. As I walked through the back door I thought I would play it cool, but alas couldn't contain myself half hoping for poppers and streamers and a house full of friendly faces. Disappointedly Mum was the only one in the house and seemed genuinely happy for me, but she wasn't her normal self and I knew then that she had already been told not show too much interest. To say my enthusiasm was flattened was an understatement and the welcoming committee of one brought me crashing back down to earth.

Dad had already made his feelings known, so Mum had the unenviable task of doing as Dad had ordered her to do by not encouraging me but also be pleased for me at the same time. It's hard for me to know what I had put Mum through; I certainly didn't choose the work experience to make her life any harder than it already was, but I also knew that nothing ever lasts forever and things do change, people change, circumstances change and from time to time hard decisions and sacrifices have to be made even if it does upset a few apple carts along the way. In hindsight my Mum was my real hero, I just never realised it at the time and if I knew it would have made her life easier I would have quit the job there and then. I didn't, not because it would have given Dad the opportunity to gloat saying *'I told you so'* but because I really felt like I needed to do this and rubber stamp my own identity.

I knew Mum was proud of me without her even saying a word. She was proud of all her kids and whatever they did. She showed no prejudice or found fault with anyone, ever. Frustratingly nor too did she ever stand her corner, and many a time I so wished she would for once just say no, but for the families sake never did. In later years, when it was too late, I began to understand why she was like she was, and why she did what she did. In my eyes, albeit a life of psychological oppression, she was an absolute angel. Simply put, Mum lived whole heartedly for her family; nothing else mattered. It didn't matter to her what world events were going on or what wars were being fought, her world was there within her four walls. Mars or Venus could have been the next town down but she wasn't interested about anything else apart from the most important thing in her life – her family. She proved to me as I matured into an adult that it takes a much stronger person to hold on to a loose tongue and not say something I might later regret. I used to think it was Mum that had the insecurities because of her placid introvert nature but as I grew older and a little wiser I began to understand that she was in fact far stronger than Dad and his unpredictable explosive tempers. All the same it wasn't fair and it certainly wasn't right, but Mum knew her place and I think she had accustomed her mind and spirit to be elsewhere when family life wasn't so pleasant.

Well, so much for the welcoming committee – a party of one! But at least it was the most important person to me. It's funny what people's perceptions of Undertaking are. Dad's main gripe was that I would bring bugs and diseases home; that it wasn't right, and if he had his way, I should probably have been sent away to a *funny farm* for re evaluation of my mind. Dad was of Eastern European descent and had gone through hard times, survived extreme poverty, abused childhood mentally and physically and an uprising in his homeland; he had escaped certain death for those being sent to be executed and in turn did what he had to do to escape his troubled and turbulent past. Dad took it personally that I chose to do what I was doing and couldn't understand why anyone especially his first born having an interest in death when he had suffered so much agony and turmoil of his own in his native Hungary. This is why Dad could not accept what I was doing; to him this was personal as if I were driving a knife through him. Of course, I wasn't, I was just finding myself, but to him it was unnatural, and that was that! In some way I imagined Mum would get the blame for me turning out the way I was and that she had somehow failed as a Mother.

For the rest of the family, it was all fairly low key not knowing whether to engage in conversation for the fear of what I might say. For everyone else, it was the start of every joke I have ever heard a thousand times over since. Needless to say, my advice now is unless you have the full support of the people that matter around you, think very carefully about doing what I did.

6. Back for more

The next morning came and I couldn't wait to get going and without so much as a bye or leave I was off to work. Excitedly and in good time with a spring in my step, I entered the estate, walked into the gatehouse and looked for my name on the clock card rack, punched my ticket and walked the short distance to the coffin shop. The door was open and the lads were already reposed in their given chairs exchanging banter, supping tea and of course smoking fags.

'Not sure whether you'd be back Jan' said Roy. *'No worries there – I had a good time yesterday'*.

Pleasantries aside, as with every morning, the worksheets from the office for the days funerals were handed out to each of us and the duties we were responsible for for the day (who was driving the hearse, limousine, timings of when and where we had to be on the funerals etc. etc). Naturally my name wasn't on the sheets, and to be honest I felt a little left out, but in all fairness, I was only there for the experience for the week.

Roy had given me a list of things to do in their absence, which I didn't mind as I would at least be able to get on in my own pace without anyone looking over my shoulder, and the reassurance of what I had done the day before meant that Roy trusted me enough to have a go at furnishing the coffins on my own. *'Don't worry if you get stuck Jan. I'll help you out when I get back'* he said. *'I'll see what I can do for you by the end of the week to give you something else to try'.*

Once the lads had finished their brew they made their way and said they would be back soon. The lads drove off in the hearse and limousine past the gatehouse to the chapel and mortuary that was a short distance from the estate in its own private grounds where they would prepare and load the coffin on to the back of the hearse for the funeral of the day.

I knew what was expected of me and was left to my own intuition. It was important for me to make a good impression and I wanted to get it right. For the most part with trial and error I did, and soon got the hang of lining coffins with no effort. I had finished well before the lads got back, and so decided to pop into the canteen. I had no money on me, just enough for my bus fare home, but nor did I actually go in for anything to eat, just to be nosey. The lady behind the counter reminded me of one of those dinner ladies you had at school (slightly on the plump side, a permed blue rinse and a motherly smile). *'What can I do for you?'* she asked. *'I was just looking'.* *'Well while you're here you may as well have a sit down and a drink'.* *'I'm sorry, I can't'* too embarrassed to say I had no money on me. *'That's okay, this one's on the house'.* Gratefully I received a hot mug of chocolate which was most welcome. She asked me how I was settling in and did her best with small talk to make me feel at ease. In return I tried not to give too many one word answers as I wasn't sure what I was supposed to say. Once I had drunk my drink, I thanked her and said I would see her tomorrow.

Roy, Colin, Tony and Reg rolled in from the day's funeral all pleased with themselves exchanging the usual banter. *'Got the kettle on Jan?'* they said together, as if they need ask. Roy made a bee line to see what I had done and was pleased with my efforts and naturally as I expected made some minor adjustments, even though there was nothing wrong with it. I was fine with this, and I could see he was pleased.

Before leaving that day, Roy had informed me that there would be a lorry delivering 50 headstones and 50 bases the next day and that if the delivery turned up before they were back, to just wait for them and make the driver a drink. I could take it from that comment that I was going to be kept in the coffin shop again which was fine as I was enjoying finding my way around the workshop and the estate anyway.

The following day, quite predictably the delivery turned up as the lads were out on a funeral. I had told the driver what Roy had said to me, but he was in need of getting away, and so began to unload on his own. I could hardly watch him struggle and not help, and so I did. I don't need to tell anyone how heavy headstones are. The bases alone are weighty enough and should require two people to handle safely. The space in the garage was already clear for the stones, so it was simply a case of off the back of the lorry and into the garage. Now bear in mind I was only 16 years old and despite being in the school rugby team was a very small 16 year old - 7 stone wet and the physique of a pepperami. Being the hands on sort I was, I helped the driver to offload. I think after the first couple of stones, I realised that it probably wasn't the brightest idea particularly after what Roy had told me, but once started I could hardly disappear for a tea break; in any case it's just not in my genetic make up to get out of doing something.

I had visualised what Colin would have done in this situation if he had been on his own. I imagined he would have quite deliberately lifted one stone awkwardly and conveniently feigned a muscle pull and have to sit down for a fag and a cup of tea.

Even with the aid of the pump truck, it was hard work and thankfully a delivery like that didn't happen every day. Predictably, the lads rolled in through the gates just as I had helped unload the last headstone. Roy was none too pleased at the driver for letting me help with the delivery for fear I could have injured myself and how that might look on the work experience report when I went back to school. Colin, Tony and Reg on the other hand were more than grateful the hard work had been done; Colin smiled and was more delighted than anyone.

Thursday came and it was decided that I had earned a change of scenery. This was to be my first real baptism of fire in the profession. Colin had been instructed to go to one of the cottage hospitals just on the outskirts of town to collect a lady from their mortuary. Nothing untoward and one that the office thought might be a good test for me. Never having seen a dead person in my life, all of a sudden the clarity of what I was doing here suddenly became very real. Adrenaline overload or panic? I wasn't sure, but I had to look as if this was something I had done a thousand times before, just as Colin had. Colin explained that the old cottage hospitals were much less formal and busy unlike the main hospitals of the bigger towns and cities. They were generally friendlier places than the main hospitals and more laid back, everyone knew everyone else by name and generally ranks and titles didn't demine or uphold anyone. *'A team is a team'* Colin said which was quite rich coming from someone that if he were a footballer would have been quite happy sitting on the subs bench every week. The first port of call was the reception to arrange for a porter to let us into 'Rose Cottage' a name commonly known as the mortuary in all the hospitals locally. Next a short drive to the rear of the hospital where we parked in the ambulance bay next to the mortuary to await the Porter. There was nothing unusual about the appearance of the small red bricked building, nothing that would have drawn you to think what it must be; save the plaque on the door reading Chapel of Repose. Cottage hospitals generally had refrigeration spaces for up to 4 bodies purely because these hospitals were quite small and there was no need for anything bigger. Over the years, even when you travel to a hospital mortuary you have never been to before you get an instinct as to where the mortuary is, almost like a tracker unit built into you, don't ask me how you know, you just do.

The Porter and Colin rambled away without a care in the world. I on the other hand kept my distance a couple of feet back as they pulled out the tray which the deceased, wrapped in a cloth shroud was lying on. The transfer from tray to stretcher was effortless as they carried on their chat. It was a very surreal moment and I could feel my jaw drop in disbelief that while Colin and the Porter were passing the time of day; there in front of me lay a dead body. I must admit, I never knew what to expect, but the relaxed manner and controlled environment made it far easier than I had expected, that and the fact that I didn't know the person.

The ease of everything that had just taken place in no more than a couple of minutes was as if the lady didn't exist. Of course she did, but as Colin had explained to me, *'This was part of everyday life. We accept it. There is nothing disrespectful by us carrying on in our usual manner, we have to, otherwise we would all end up in the local mental hospital. Keep an open mind about everything and always expect the unexpected. Stick to that and you'll be alright'.* Sound advice from someone that didn't like working for a living but he was right, and despite his lethargic ways, he knew his job, even if it did take twice as long as everyone else.

The final day came almost too quickly, and I had spotted on the worksheet for the day that it included me as one of the pallbearers on the funeral. It was to be a small affair with only a handful of mourners expected. The hearse was spotless and ready to go. Roy, Tony and Reg would meet us at the crematorium as there was no need for a following car.

The funeral director Mr Reeves arrived at the coffin shop for the debrief. This was a rundown of who the service was for and instructions if any that we might need to know such as who the vicar was, what hymns were being sung if any, where the flowers were to go after the service etc. Once debriefed and everyone looking their part we all jumped into the hearse – the Funeral Director naturally in the front passenger seat. As we drove the short distance to the gatehouse past the other departments on the estate, the Gateman lifted the barrier removed his hat and respectfully held his head low as we drove past, a ritual he performed on a daily basis. I wasn't sure whether this was his mark of respect or just a private joke between him and the drivers as he would also give the them a toothless grin on our going out and coming in. Whatever the reason, it felt special; I felt special.

A sharp turn left and then left again took us into the chapel and mortuary where once checked, the coffin and flowers were loaded and off we went direct to the crematorium. As we travelled, I couldn't help feeling important as the hearse always attracted the attention of onlookers and mostly commanded the respect among fellow drivers (something very rarely seen nowadays). As the hearse pulled up under the canopy to the chapel doors the reality hit me like a sledgehammer. This wasn't a trial run, this was the real deal. All I had been briefed about and what to do was racing around in my head like a gyroscope, and as simple as the instructions were, I kept hoping I wouldn't mess it up. As I stood at the back of the hearse with Colin, Roy and Tony I could feel my heart racing with adrenaline; my mouth started to dry up as if I was chewing on a car sponge. I wasn't about to let the team down, but more importantly I was not about to let myself down. Reg was there to step in as a precautionary measure if I changed my mind. This was however my last day, and I was determined to see the week out with honours.

I partnered Roy on the foot end (the front), Colin and Tony on the head. Once clear of the back door on the hearse and still underarm, waited for the count of three from the Director and lifted together onto our shoulders. My legs were now weak and jelly like, not because the coffin was heavy, but because I was as nervous as hell. All I had to remember was to start off on the left foot. I mean how hard can it be to remember that one thing? Well, as silly as it sounds I did remember; how much of it was luck and how much was intentional is irrelevant, it was after all a 50/50 chance. The coffin was never going to slip between us as Roy always linked arms with his opposite. I never felt comfortable with that way of carrying as it always seemed far too camp. If that wasn't bad enough I knew of a bearer that used to put his arm around the other bearers waist – now that really did look like some serious mincing. It was a short walk down the aisle and gently off the shoulder where the coffin then took its place on the catafalque (a platform where the coffin is on view to the mourners). We all then faced the coffin, bowed and turned to the congregation to await the signal of the director to take our seats. There could not have been more than half a dozen people there and as I looked over to the few that were sat there on the oak pews, felt saddened that at the end of a life, there were just a handful of people here to say goodbye. Surely that person must have known more than six people?

This was far more commonplace than you might think, sometimes because there are no family left, or the person had outlived everyone they knew or even on occasion it was a specific wish that there was to be no one present, not even a vicar. Every funeral director has their own way of conducting funerals and it was company policy for the director and bearers to sit through the service and accompany singing if needed. Singing is NOT my forte and listening to the others nor was theirs, but that's another story. The service came to a close and the congregation filed out behind the director and vicar followed by us taking up the rear. Roy showed me where to collect the flowers from in the back chamber of the crematorium. This is the holding chamber between chapel and cremator where final checks are made to confirm the nameplate details are correct with the crematorium worksheets. All responsibility for the reception of the deceased from the funeral director passes over to the crematorium once we enter the chapel. Here I met all too briefly the crematory operator who was like most of the people I had met all week the sort I could spend a lot of time with even if not today.

The flowers were then laid out in the garden of remembrance on a marker that had the deceased name on it. Once the mourners had seen the flowers, after a few more minutes thanked us all and left. This was our job done, and I felt as if I had been part of something really important.

Back at the yard, Mr Compton was waiting to see how I had fared. Mr Reeves and the lads were very complimentary about my performance, and I in turn thanked Mr Compton for having me for a truly great week, and asked if he might consider me again should any opportunities arise.

7. School for the last time

I was sure no one would come close to topping the week I had, and I suppose for the first time ever, apart from PE, I was actually looking forward to Monday morning and going to school - a shame it wasn't until the last month of my school life before I didn't find it a chore.

Don't get me wrong, school and education is important, but regrettably it wasn't for me. The education system and me were like two opposing poles of a magnet; school didn't like me and I didn't like it. I rebelled against the system pretty much the whole time I was there. I can recall Monday morning assemblies usually ended on a predictable sour note with my name amongst the other usual suspects being retained in the head teachers' office for the detentions we were to receive for one mischief or another from the previous week.

School in all its glory meant nothing to me and certainly wasn't the best years of my life. I had at least now gone the distance, and only a short term left with some exams to fill in and that would end a chapter forever. I am pretty certain as misguided as I was, that the teachers didn't give me an awful lot of hope and would probably not amount to much. I didn't really care what the teachers or anyone thought. I knew even then I was different from everyone else, just not sure how? My weeks work experience was just the first of many doors that opened that showed me who I was.

Needless to say, I had all sorts of questions from everyone about the week that I had just done, mostly obvious ones from the rest of the last year pupils like *'Did you see a dead person?'* and *'What did they look like?'* the usual morbid interest. I could go on, but I think you get the drift; when you've heard the same thing for the first hundred times or so, it starts to wear thin and gets a bit boring as you politely force a smile. I don't think in all the five years there I had had so much interest paid to me. At least the Careers Officer was less obvious with his questioning, asking about the staff, the work conditions and how I felt. How did I feel? On top of the world actually. I really did enjoy the week at my placement. The grind of school life over the last eleven years was at last paling into insignificance. I could see the Careers Officer was genuinely interested in my answers as it was also a first for him. In time, my experiences opened the flood gates for many, many others that had work placements in Undertakers.

I didn't let things rest there neither and called the funeral directors a few times over the next few weeks looking for some more opportunities to go back. Politely they said that at that time they had nothing to give me but encouraged me to keep trying. Frustratingly I had found something I really enjoyed doing, but there was no opening, and certainly none of the smaller firms would be able to help either.

I remember being at home one afternoon watching the telly when the telephone rang. *'Mum!...phone'* I called as I was too engrossed with something far more important on the box. *'It's for you'* she said, *'Who is it?'* I asked inquisitively as no one ever called me. *'The funeral directors'*, *'Hang on'* I said as I jumped out of my seat losing half my tea down my front. Mr Compton had said that they were pleased with my efforts and willingness to learn and had liked my attitude towards everyone else. He went on to say that if I was interested they would make an opening for an apprentice funeral operative if I was still keen? *'Yes please'* I said excitedly. *'When?'* Mr Compton replied *'Monday if it doesn't cause any problem with your school'*. *'It won't'* I said, not knowing whether it would or not but that didn't really matter.

At this point Mum had worked out for herself what I had been offered and was quietly pleased for me. She wanted me to be happy and was happy that I had a job to go to but also realised that the hard part was breaking the news to Dad and convincing him that it was better than nothing. *'Leave him to me'* she said sighing under her breath convincing me it would be okay.

Now when the shit hits the fan in our house, it really hits it – no prisoners. No time was going to be a good time to break this sort of news. Predictably Dad was a man possessed at this bombshell and was fuming with rage as if I had deliberately set out to wind him up. Mum tried in vain to convince him that at least I had a job. *'That is not a job!'* He roared *'He's had his fun – now he must go and get a proper job'*. A few doors slammed and that was that; everyone just kept out of each other's way. The atmosphere was pretty dire for a long time to come after that and I wondered what I had put Mum through? She didn't deserve to be piggy in the middle and I was responsible for it. I am sure Dad felt it was some personal vendetta against him and that I was just going through a rebellious stage in my life. He was convinced I would bring ill home and that I had brought shame to the whole family darkening a black cloud over his threshold. I had in his eyes failed. As much as this hurt, I couldn't let it go and I knew I would pay the consequences for my stubbornness. This wasn't the last I would hear about it; that much I knew.

As it turned out school didn't mind on the proviso I told my new employer I had to be released to do my one remaining 'O' level technical drawing exam. In truth this made the school look good as well as it proved what a valuable department the work experience program was and not just cheap labour for uninterested employers. Quite an achievement considering the bleak outlook that some had for me. Looking back now, a lot of the lads that left in my year that had less than favourable reports ended up working for themselves and eventually becoming successful business men.

8. My new 9-5 job

Well, in truth it was, initially anyway. That was until I would be old enough to go on call when I reached eighteen. The job was for real this time, and I was getting paid £ 25.00 per week for it! To put this into perspective most 16 year olds were on £ 25.00 per week, so it was nothing out of the ordinary, even if the job was. At that time the rest of the lads were on about £ 80.00 per week plus call outs and out of hour's duties. By this time I had my very own Garelli moped that I bought out of money I had earned from various weekend jobs gardening for the 'Rich' people around the lanes, selling Sweet William flowers from our garden in the redundant lay-by that once was a bus stop (mighty damn glad no one ever asked if I had a licence for this). Elvering time on the banks of the River Severn was another source of pocket money. That was a time when you would come back with bucket loads of elvers unlike today when you'd be lucky to return with a cup full. After loading our haul into the back of the van I would be perched mantis style on the wheel arch inside my cousins Ford Escort van holding on for dear life to the dustbins part full of elvers so as not to lose our catch on the way back home. Regrettably he didn't know the meaning of taking it steady whether on the straight or around corners and this was probably more of a challenge getting back in one piece than catching the elvers on the freezing cold banks of the Severn in the first place, (thank goodness the councils hadn't introduced those ridiculous speed humps back then otherwise I would have been wearing most of them). Back in the time when elvers were plentiful and not the delicacy they are today, you were lucky to get 50 pence per pound. A lot of people around the village expected them for nothing and was probably regarded as a poor man's meal. They never tasted of anything in particular and Dad would often fry them alive mixed into an omelette for good measure. Me personally, I couldn't see the fascination in them other than how much pocket money I could make. It would be fair to say that I considered myself resourceful and if there was a way to earn a few 'Bob' I would. Of course I didn't save all of it, some weekends, as lads around the age of twelve or thirteen we would go to another part of the lanes to an old 'Scrumpy Farm'. Farmer Bob or Mr Jennings as we respectfully called him brewed his very own distinguished cider. He was a wiry seasoned old farmer no more than 5 foot in height (probably nearer six if led flat on a rack) body bent like a boomerang and legs so bowed he certainly wouldn't stop a pig in a passage, but he was a great old man of little words that was quite happy with life just the way it was. He didn't aspire to anything and certainly had no materialistic need which was evident from the simple lifestyle he had. He was always happy and smiling – I think the home brew may have contributed to this. I don't remember ever seeing him in anything other than his well worn cardboard like dungarees and open neck checked shirt he lived in day and night which for all anyone ever knew may have been the sum total of his wardrobe. Incredibly he didn't smell, at least I don't think so? Living in the countryside, not too far from the local pig farm across the field meant the air always smelled of pigs and if you were unlucky enough for the wind to be in the wrong direction which was always more prominent in the hotter summer months it was a smell that would linger in the haze for days *'Ah, the Country life I hear you say'* needless to say it wasn't ideal for hanging out your washing. Farmer Bob was always pleased to see me and Pete and always greeted us *'Afternoon boys – what will it be?'* as if he need ask. Farmer Bob always insisted we try a shot of scrumpy first and would scoop a hollowed bull horn of his finest for us to drink from. This was a ritual we always went through, not that it was ever going to taste of anything different as he just kept topping up the same oak vat year on year. The taste never got any better, but never got any worse either despite all sorts that had fallen off the over head beams into the broth over the years. To be fair the taste was disgusting; you could almost feel the hair on it as it warmed its way down your throat stripping the inner lining en route to the bed of the stomach, but once you got past the first shot it didn't seem to matter. Farmer Bob had known us since we were knee high and knew how old we were not that that mattered as he didn't have any rules barring underage drinking. The fact we had ridden our pushbikes to the farm were a giveaway sign of our youth but no harm was ever done and Farmer Bob was always grateful for the 50 pence we handed over in exchange for the gallon container of his home grown cloudy gut rot which doubled as turps for cleaning your paintbrushes when you couldn't drink any more.

I had grown up to understand the real value of money, and it was always an issue with the lack of it. I can't honestly admit to enjoying this level of communal standing, when so many of my friends and families around me seemed to be a rung or two higher. I am sure there were in reality lots of families like ours, and I guess the one thing life on this level prepares you for as you got older was that whatever you want in life, you have to go out there and get it. Unless you have been extremely lucky and had the good fortune of inheritance then like me there is only one way, and that is the hard way. I have never done anything by halves, and you only get out what you put in.

So here I was in the big wide world, working for a living. I now felt part of the team, and they were all pleased to have me back. Everything went pretty much as it did in the work experience and I slowly became more confident with the people around me, still being careful not to be too cock sure as I didn't want anyone to get the wrong impression of me. Apart from the driving, I became involved with all aspects of the job and learned as much as I could. The only way to learn in this profession is hands on because there are so many parts to the job that are one offs. Nothing can prepare you for this; no school, no training, no nothing – there is absolutely nothing to compare it with and I am sure that is the reason why so many in the profession see it as a job for life because it can be so interesting and varied. The week had gone pretty much as it did previously but with the added bonus of looking forward to my first wage packet at the end of the week. It was the assistant managers' job to come to the coffin shop to hand over our weekly dues. This was a duty that Mr Reeves considered a chore as it was a non funereal part of his job. I didn't care; it was like Christmas for me, receiving my first real wage. I rode home pretty fast that evening, more carelessly than I usually did, only because I wanted to show Mum what I had earned. You'd have thought no one had ever earned a wage in their life before the way I proudly extended my hand and showed Mum the brown envelope. She was pleased, genuinely pleased, and said that Dad had told her that I wasn't to pay any housekeep for three months, just so I could earn a bit of money. That was a shock and a half as I thought he might be coming around to the idea. He hadn't – he just didn't want to be part of it, and this was his way of showing it. Somehow he had seen it as dirty money and that I probably wouldn't last three months before getting a 'proper job' anyway.

Days, weeks and months went by, and I grew with the job. After the three months I started to pay housekeep. My wage was still £25.00. which was split into £10.00 for housekeep, £ 5.00 for petrol in my moped for the week, and a whole £ 10.00 to do with what I wanted. My family couldn't really see the fascination in what I did and so could never get excited about what day I had had as opposed to my cousin who was a farm hand who would talk about the hernia on Mabel the cow or my Uncle who was a road sweeper for the council that could tell you everything you needed to know about fly tipping. I was always astounded how talking about a bloody cow or how much rubbish had been dumped in the lay by down the road could be any more interesting than what I did. No offence to anyone that works in those respected areas, but I just didn't understand how you could talk about the same thing day in day out. Some things never change though and that was the ways things were in village life.

So here I was in the big wide world, in my 9 to 5 job earning my own money; what could possibly go wrong?

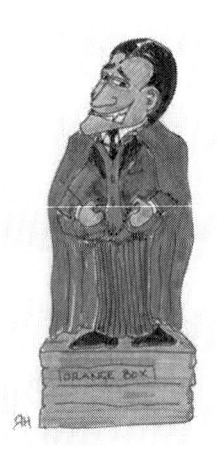

9. The Ultimatum

Fatal last words when all seems to be on the up. Dad was never going to budge on his stance about how he felt, and made it known early on that if I insisted on keeping my job, then I could not live under his roof. He was convinced more than ever that I might bring home the Bubonic plague or some other disease that would wipe out the entire family. He had this thought that you could catch cancer off people and wouldn't listen to any reasoning from me. At seventeen, things had got unbearable and I for one couldn't wait to leave home, which naturally Mum, Nan and Granddad were unhappy about. It was an easy decision for me though as I had got fed up with the negativity in the house, and I was the core reason for it. I had found great solace in work and the people I shared the day with as it was a happier friendlier place to be, even if some of the people there didn't answer back.

The upheaval of leaving home regardless of circumstance is a major event, even traumatic. I didn't exactly have to worry about packing too much, as I had no worldly goods to speak of. I had moved about 15 miles away and rented a room in a private house which was very clean and tidy. The Lady of the house also lived here and for the pitiful rent she charged, I certainly had a good deal as my meals were all inclusive too which probably meant I was living there for nothing. I got the feeling she was just more than happy to share her house with someone and that the money wasn't even an issue. She was an ex school teacher and at some point I am guessing one of the original 'Flower Power' people from the 'Swinging 60's'. Her home was a very calm home with an aromatic smell of oil burners and joss sticks, uncluttered and organised unlike the one I had come from but somehow was too clinical and sanitised which as lovely as it was, was better suited for an older person than me . Even though I had this new unbound freedom without having to concern myself over anyone else's views I felt slightly awkward in the company of my Landlady – not for anything she said or did, as she was truly accommodating in every way but because I felt that I had nothing in common with her and conversation I found difficult particularly as she was well read and a mind of information about everything.

As contradictory as this may sound and as lovely as the new surroundings were...it wasn't home. Don't get me wrong, I hated home life and the problems that came with it, but as far as stepping out of the fire and into the frying pan I had gone from one extreme to another and decided that I needed to move closer to home again and try to find a happy medium.

At least I had taken my first major step into the big outdoors and a move back home was simply out of the question. I had broken the chain once, and as hard as things were, that was the way it had to be – not that I was ever asked to come back home anyway.

At work there was a major reshuffle in management as Mr Compton had decided to take a position within the group down South. He had considered this a good move and we all wished him well. I for one was very sorry to see him leave. If I had known what was about to come I would have clung to his tail coat and begged him to stay.

Donald Reeves had been groomed for this position for years, and so he was rightfully upset that the reshuffle had brought in a new manager to replace Mr Compton. Don was to stay as assistant to the manager which didn't go down too well and caused a lot of forced resentment.

The day of the new manager came and we were all called together for a group meeting to greet Mr Peter McCann. Mr McCann was brought in to shake things up and bring about change, (This happens quite a lot from time to time in larger companies when the higher echelons decide things have become stagnant – a bit like rebranding, but instead of company logos you rebrand and retrain your staff). Mr McCann had a Trade Union background and knew everything there was to know about employment law, so there was no pulling the wool over his eyes. He was totally business minded and focused about how a company should be run and would always get the most from his staff even if it did ruffle a few feathers. He had an aura that was brimming with arrogance and had no qualms about setting out his stall on how things would run under his leadership.

As Mr McCann took centre stage in the front office, head angled back and looking down the bridge of his nose with incredible importance he announced proudly as if giving a party political speech 'I am Mr McCann'. I knew as soon as he said this, that he was a man not to be messed with and that there was bound to be changes afoot. He made it abundantly clear that there would be no use of first names. Sheila was a second cousin to Mr McCann but even she would not be on first name terms with him, nor he with her as he referred to her only as Mrs Wadley. He made it very clear that work is for work, and this amongst other changes was the precedent for his reign to be. I knew from this unfortunate moment things would never be the same again and they weren't.

I had two misfortunes, firstly Mr McCann didn't like adolescents, and I was definitely one of those and secondly he had inherited me from Mr Compton along with everyone else, which he didn't bear well either. The latter affected all of us, and so until things settled down, we all just got along trying not to upset him, as we knew he was sent to shake a few trees. Sheila had said that even though he was her cousin, not even she would ever trust him and cemented the fact that he was a man that would have no conscience about shopping his own mother if it meant climbing a few rungs on the corporate ladder. I think Mr McCann misread the title when he applied for the job as Director mistaking it for Dictator. The latter he was top of the class for, and yet despite all the things I really didn't like about him he was an absolute genius when it came to organising people and for that he was second to none which I assume is why he got the position.

Mr McCann was always razor sharp and had a tongue to match if you fell on the wrong side of him, which made me pitiful for anyone on the backlash of his wrath should anyone dare cross him. Strange that he should end up being a Funeral Manager considering his apparent lack of empathy towards clients, but for some reason families liked and respected him, even when he was damn right rude.

I was the junior and knew that Mr McCann would never really warm to me as the others had, so I just had to keep my nose clean and stay out of his way as much as I could. At the end of the day regardless of who was cracking the whip at the top I was still doing a job I liked, in any case knowing how the group worked, the top job only ever carried a shelf life of 5 years or so, 10 if you were lucky, so for Don Reeves he was probably in a better position than Mr McCann even if he had felt betrayed by the society.

10. My First Real Test

As much as you can ever learn, either from text book or what life changing experiences come knocking at your door, nothing can ever prepare you for the loss of someone close whether it was expected or not. I had for now witnessed firsthand and was privy to the delicate and eggshell frailty of mortal pain on a daily basis. You do as a matter of necessity desensitise from being drawn into any sort of emotion. Families rely on the experience of the Funeral Director to make proceedings run as smoothly as possible without anyone having to concern themselves with anything other than mourning the person that had died. Desensitising doesn't mean not caring! We all hurt from time to time, and need someone to depend on, and I believe this is the true value of a good Funeral Director. As someone once said to me, finding a good Funeral Director was like finding a good Doctor and if you are lucky enough to know one, embrace them like one of the family – they will never let you down.

If a family holds you in this light, then you have been truly blessed as I have been many times over the years.

It would be impossible never to be drawn in to the emotional side of death, and it usually happens when your guard is down. Whenever children are involved, it is understandably a tense and draining time for everyone. Without question, this is the one part of the job I just wish never happened. At those intervals in my professional life I just wanted to be anywhere but there. All you want to do is say the right words and put things right, but sometimes you can't and life can be very very cruel. There is never any justification for the loss of a young one and I bet you couldn't find a single word in the English dictionary that would come anywhere near close to how someone feels at that moment.

Pete was my best friend for as long as I can remember. We lived in the same village and did everything together ever since we could walk. We went to the same Toddler group, Primary School and then Secondary. I was proud to have a true friend like him, and even when we went separate ways after School with our jobs, we still managed to have one last trip to Weymouth for a camping holiday with three other mates Dave, Mart and Tim that also lived in the village. Mart used his racing green 1969 ford escort, with me as co driver that housed the camping equipment while Pete, Dave and Tim convoyed behind on their respective 250cc motorbikes. We arrived at the cliff side site nice and early and successfully pitched our six man tent in no time at all. I could only imagine what the rest of the serious campers thought of us as we playfully larked around. The view out to the English Channel from our high point was quite stunning with nothing more than a haze on the horizon and a rising sun that beamed across the bay.

Just as night fell, the biggest almighty thunder storm came crashing down on us. Initially it was all a bit of fun and we did our best to carry on drinking and playing cards. The tent began to shake violently by the hurricane force gale that had now started to give us concern for our own safety. The canvas sheet that was still just reminiscent of the tent we had erected only a few hours earlier was now starting to lose shape as the storm continued to batter the site. One by one the guy ropes loosened their hold and was now barely serving any purpose at all, and what we had believed to be a waxed canvas turned out to be as waterproof as a straw hat. The rain cascaded in like a waterfall totally ruining the base sheet, sleeping bags and everything else in a matter of minutes. Eventually conceding to the inevitable we salvaged what we could and retreated to the brick laundry room a few yards away with the rest of the campers. From the safe haven of the laundry room we could see the magnificence of the lightning bolts as they danced across the Channel like banshees with intermittent brilliant white sheet lightning silhouetting the whole of the bay.

The whole night was spent drying out and spending what few pounds we had left in the overworked tumble dryers. Morning came and as we looked over to where we had been just a few hours before the full extent to how bad the storm had been was clear to all. Our tent had now taken up refuge on the Cliffside hedgerow 100 yards away. Realising how lucky we were to have escaped from what could have been a very dangerous situation we packed up and left somewhat wounded from our adventure which sadly unbeknown at the time was to be the last.

We arrived back home on the Sunday and said our goodbyes somewhat deflated by our ordeals. That was the last time I had seen my best friend Pete and had had no contact with him after then as we all had our own busy lives to carry on with. The next time I had heard anything about Pete was that he was now in a steady relationship and had been dating a girl he had known from school for the last year who was also six months pregnant and naturally looking forward to Fatherhood. I had popped up to Mum's house one weekend shortly after I heard the news about Pete and his girlfriend and to catch up with him as we hadn't seen each other since Weymouth.

I was always pleased to see Mum, as she was me, but her head was hung low with sadness as I walked in. I knew it was the face of bad news, and I could tell she didn't really want to be the bearer of it. *'What's the matter Mum?' 'It's Pete'* she said *'he died a couple of days ago'*. She must be wrong I thought as my heart sank like a heavy paperweight – people don't just die. When the shock started to filter through to my brain the realisation of what she was telling became overwhelming. I sat down lifeless and numb on the chair staring into space; my body trying to adjust to a million and one emotions. I understood firsthand shock and the pains of grief, and I felt physically sick and empty. My one and only true friend died aged 20 and I didn't even get chance to say goodbye.

11. Ship of the desert

Of course there are times that not everything goes to plan or occasionally events happen outside of the Funeral Directors control. Thank goodness some of these events happened before mobile phone cameras were invented.

The funeral of a long distance Lorry Driver was to take place at a church close by. As expected because of the circles he had kept there would be a large congregation.

Booted and suited we were all ready to go, everything was in place and there was nothing out of the ordinary that anyone should be aware of. The interesting part of our job, is that you can cross all the t's and dot all the i's but there will from time to time be occasions where the unexpected will happen.

Reverend Thomas presiding was an interesting vicar that quite often went off on tangents leaving the congregation wondering if indeed he was even attending the right service. Initially I had trouble following his sermons and would usually find my head dropping no soon as I had sat down.

When I cottoned on to his analogies and similes I soon realised he was actually a very good story teller, which to be fair is a rare talent that a lot of clergy could learn from. On the downside though, he was hopelessly useless at timekeeping even though he lived in the vicarage next door.

I don't think there was ever an occasion he would be in the doorway to the church waiting. For us it was common practice to arrive in good time, and then politely explain to the family that you just needed to let the vicar know we were there. Even then he would still manage to delay proceedings a few more minutes. When he did finally stroll across the yard to the church, his over cloak was invariably covered in feathers from the Canadian geese he kept as pets in the front garden.

Reverend Thomas always more than made up for his poor timekeeping and slight eccentricity by giving you a truly personal service and for that reason alone was popular with families and funeral directors alike.

He would never give you a short answer to anything, so if you were looking for directions from A to B then he would take you via C, D and E exactly the same as he would do with all of his sermons too.

After the welcome and introduction Reverend Thomas then continued to talk about Bactrian Camels. These are the two humped Camels that roam the Gobi Desert and Steppes of Asia. This was not unusual for an opening from Reverend Thomas as he usually went off on some fantastic story leaving you wondering if indeed he even had the right address.

The vague relevance to this funeral was that Reverend Thomas likened the long distance Lorry Driver to that of the Bactrian camel – a strange simile to use in a funeral service I know, and probably would have been more suited on a different occasion, but interesting none the less.

He had said that for long periods both camel and lorry driver would need to stock up on reserves for the journey ahead, that both led solitary and at times nomadic lifestyles in unknown territories and travelled great distances. All of his sermons were like this and you were often left wondering if he would ever get to the point of where it was all leading.

Just as Reverend Thomas was getting into full swing about the life and times of the Bactrian camel, a young Mother and baby entered through the back door – late for whatever reason. As she tried to close the door quietly the spring loaded door pulled to making a loud slam, which simultaneously made everyone look around. The only seat left was on the front pew which the verger ushered her to. Unperturbed by her entrance and momentarily halting proceedings, Reverend Thomas continued his talk about the Bactrian camel only to be silenced seconds later by the young Mother who in full view of the whole congregation and himself pull out one of her heavily laden mammaries for breastfeeding.

Reverend Thomas was finally at a loss for words as his jaw dropped, and everyone including the family broke the revered silence with muffled tittering. I wondered if Reverend Thomas would have been saved his blushes if he'd based his sermon on the Dromedary Camel instead. The hymn followed immediately and I am sure the babies thoughts were probably *'for what we are about to receive, make us truly grateful. Amen'*.

12. Dust to Dust

An early memory I have was of a vicar who was definitely not the typical stereotype. He called a spade a spade and openly admitted he was like marmite as you either loved him or hated him – he knew this, and thrived on the fact he was controversial.

He had a knack of being able to push you to the limits of your patience just to see if he could get a reaction out of you, in fact if truth had it he wasn't happy unless he could get you biting. Nonetheless, he meant well even if his practice and ministry was somewhat unorthodox.

Reverend Gordon Evans was well known locally for his ability to hold his own for drinking at one of many local watering holes and also enjoyed the pleasure of his pipe.

Whenever a service was held at his church he would always walk the short distance to the gates puffing on his pipe where the funeral directors and family were waiting.

As he led the procession into Church he would continue drawing away on his pipe while reciting the opening sentences.

'I am the resurrection and the life saith the Lord' coughing and spluttering intermittently between words, then just as we were about to go through the Church door he would draw one final deep drag on his pipe before placing it on the porch window ready to pick up on exit at the end of the service. He was at least respectful in that way, not taking the pipe inside that is, after all there are lines that even vicars daren't cross.

It was quite usual while the service was going on for the bearers to wait outside until the commendation and committal took place signalling the end of the service before going back in. In the 20 minutes or so of waiting outside, it was an opportunity to sometimes but not always payback the compliment with a little mischievous fun of our own with the vicar, and so it was that when the tobacco had gone out, one of us would unplug the pipe and add a small amount of sawdust from the porch window, then replace the spent tobacco on top for good measure so that he was none the wiser on his return.

I don't think the vicar ever cottoned on to our misdemeanours, and nobody as far as I am aware ever told him. The silver lining to this story though is that some months later of us adding our unbranded make of pipe tobacco, Reverend Evans decided to give up smoking.

So as far as I am concerned, even when it's not intentional, you can do good Christian acts to others without even knowing it. Granted on these occasions we did have to go to Church as well, but as I always say, you can never do enough for a good vicar.

13. Summer in Winter

One of the many funerals that I remember for one reason or another was one bitterly cold winters day. Winter can be quite hair raising when driving around in cars on the ice and snow let alone 20 foot long hearses and limousines way before the days of traction control (this was before climate change and global warming when seasons were seasons).

Automatic cars in slippery conditions are not much fun for driver or passenger, and it would always take some precision driving not to snake out the back end of the vehicle or perform ring donuts in the snow - that was saved until after the funeral back at the yard; and it's not just the driving as the bearing of coffins also required a steady hand and an awful lot of trust on the other three not slipping. If one slips, we all slip. This has happened before to others in the trade that I know but thankfully it is one mishap I have never had to deal with.

On this day, there was no let up with the snow as it came down the size and shape of golf balls and was settling fast, (not that uncommon a few years ago when I was a lad). The village I was brought up in would often get a blanket of snow over night come winter and the hills all around were beautifully picturesque with snow covered trees as if dusted with icing sugar and yet despite the dangerous driving conditions always brought a festive feel to the season.

Our biggest concern for this funeral was the travel, as we would be going to a small village on top of one of the surrounding hills. Mr McCann on this occasion abandoned his No1 shoes in favour for a pair of wellington boots and suggested we all do the same. Somehow as practical as it was it just seemed wrong and inappropriate to turn up to someone's house with a team of bearers wearing knee length wellies.

As we were all making the final preparations to leave, Mr McCann pulled on his wellies with the pressed pin stripe trousers tucked inside. Much to my amusement I couldn't resist a titter, which was not taken well and the glare of disapproval from him stopped me full in my tracks. Without further ridicule he thought better of the idea and decided to edge the trouser bottoms over the tops of the wellies which ended up looking like a pair of upside down jodhpurs. I had already retreated to a safe distance of not allowing my humour to be heard but alas it didn't stop the rest of the lads exploding into rapturous laughter which riled Mr McCann all the more, but as they were all far more senior than me in age and united in vocal spirit they were allowed the joke; I knew just to keep quiet and say nothing.

Realising this too was also inappropriate and now angered by the less than professional larking around by the lads took hold of a Stanley knife and slashed the wellies in half turning them into ankle boots. Determined to make a point it was time to stop, after all no one wanted to get on the wrong side of the boss as you knew he could make your life very unpleasant indeed if he wanted to and you wouldn't want to be at the end of his wrath.

Naturally, we had allowed extra travel time for this journey and did arrive at the house in plenty of time. Mr McCann stepped out of the hearse in his newly fashioned anti skid footwear and walked up the snow covered path to the door to advise the family that we should leave as soon as they were ready. There was no let up in the snow and I think if truth had it we were quite keen to make a move as well.

After a few minutes one of the mourners stepped out from the front door taking in the now blizzardous conditions in nothing more than a brightly coloured short sleeve shirt and pair of shorts before slipping back behind closed doors. Totally confused we all looked at each other, smiled and just assumed he was running late. Mr McCann was about to knock the door again when the door opened and out filed were the house full of mourners all wearing Hawaiian shirts, shorts and sandals; some carrying inflatable's.

It was a wish of their Father upon his demise that as the family had enjoyed many holidays together in their villa in Spain it would be only fitting that this last request be honoured. For his funeral he just wanted to spread a little ray of summer sunshine; ironic that it should be on the coldest day of the year.

I think Mr McCann could be forgiven his bad dress sense for this day as our amusement quickly focussed on the mourners and their Hawaiian shirts. This was one of my first memories of a funeral service of a difference but by no means the last.

14. Slow, Slow, Quick Quick Slow

Not too far from our chapels was the City Institution that had not got a very favourable reputation. As institutions go, it was very stereotypical of what you might expect; the clinical smell of bleached corridors, bars on windows, all staff dressed in white cloaks and paint flaking off the walls.

I don't think anyone ever looked forward to going there on removals as it always left you feeling drained and uneasy at the life the patients were subjected to. This was my first time there and Roy certainly succeeded in putting the frighteners on me as we made our way there, minding me to stay close at all times whilst inside.

Slightly concerned by this but not showing it, I felt sure it was nothing more than a windup; my mind however still subliminally allowing itself to get carried away fearing the worst. The hospital wards were accessed by an old outdated Victorian lift, the sort with two concertinaed iron gates that screeched along the runners as you opened and shut them just like someone scraping their nails down a blackboard.

We wheeled our two man stretcher into the lift, closed the gates, pressed the button and off it went. Anyone with any sort of phobia of lifts would not have felt too reassured in this one as it juddered every inch to the first floor. As the lift laboured its way up the shaft, the increasing audible sound of the patients became quite unnerving. Roy amused himself as he could see the colour start to drain from my face with every second. *'It's not as bad as it sounds'* he said *'this is quite normal'*.

As Roy opened the gates he said it was better to leave them open as it would stop anyone else calling the lift back down. On this occasion it proved to be an absolute Godsend. I imagined a lot of films had taken their inspirations from places like these. The patients were not necessarily violent or disturbed, just institutionalised where they had spent their whole lives locked away from the outside world.

Normality to them was a life of OCD, rocking backwards and forwards in chairs, random outbursts of shouting and swearing or just repeatedly chanting in a loop like a record stuck on a scratch, some would even think they were animals and crow like cockerels or bark like dogs. This disturbed me a lot as I wondered just how un stimulated they were to act like that. To the outside world this is not normal, but this was all they knew with nothing to compare it to and were basically left to their own solitary devices. As always there was no shortage of nurses to hand but none really seemed to be overly interested in what was going on; only to supervise and bring about calm when things got out of hand. We had arrived around lunchtime and some of the patients were still eating in the dining area. We had to walk through where they were still eating, which made me feel quite awkward. I had said to Roy that this didn't seem quite right, but he had told me this was the only way. The male nurse also added that they wouldn't even know what we were there for. As we walked through the dining area I was amazed to see that all of the patients were left to their own unsupervised eating habits which didn't require the use of any kind of cutlery. The unsurprising result of limited hand eye coordination ended in the usual food stuffs being scattered across the dining room floor. What little was eaten, half as much again covered their faces like an edible food mask.

The male nurse showed us to the relative calm of the ward and behind the drawn curtain lay the deceased to whom we had come to remove. There were no interruptions as we carried out our duties and once safely strapped on, we then made our way back through the dining hall. If it wasn't bad enough walking through with an empty stretcher before, it felt completely wrong going back again with a body onboard.

How strange that I should remember the sound of my feet as I squelched over the food debris, in particular the peas that crunched and popped underfoot and the mashed potato trail that carried my size 9 footprints through the hall.

It wasn't the sort of place you would want to be in any longer than you had to, and I for one was glad to get out as soon as possible. As we walked through the corridor towards the lift Roy had noticed one of the patients started to take interest in what we were doing. For reasons unknown to us, the patient took umbrage at our presence and decided to follow us waving his arms beckoning for us to stop – we didn't; and Roy had decided to quicken his pace slightly. I thought he was only joking, but I could see that his normal expression now said otherwise. As I looked around I could see the male nurse now in pursuit of the patient. Roy decided to make haste and turned a quick walk into a speed march. The four small wheels on the stretcher shook in their castors like a speed wobble clearly not designed for any pace. The lift couldn't come quick enough, and thank goodness no one else had used it since Roy left the gates open. With not a moment too soon, we were in and Roy quickly closed both gates and pressed the button. I doubt the patient had any axe to grind, but neither of us was that eager to find out. In hindsight it was highly comical, just not at the time.

The Institution no longer exists as it was closed down a few years later. The building remains but has since undergone massive investment and refurbishment and turned into a block of exclusive 1, 2 and 3 bed apartments

15. Sabbatical

My early days within the society were all good. I had made many new friends. Two of my biggest influences then were Head Mortician Marc Lord and his right hand man Rod Grainger from the City Hospital. They took me under their wing from the start and I don't think there were ever two work colleagues I got on better with than those. Apart from his daytime job Marc was also a local celebrity in the media. He had taken a shine to me and decided to be my mentor, advisor and stylist. I had never had my hair cut in a salon in my life, having gone through childhood with salad bowl haircuts and a fringe so acutely angled that even Hitler would have approved (I'm not even joking here!). My teens weren't much better even if the fringe was now at least beginning to even off more horizontally, Dad always insisting why waste good money on something he could do just the same even though he never could. He did eventually concede to the open helmet style, classic of the 70's era which made me a little bit more acceptable, even though he constantly rebuked this style as being 'sissy'.

Marc had talked me into taking a trip one Saturday to a salon in the town. He knew all the girls there by name, as this was somewhere he frequented a lot due to his necessity of looking good and keeping up appearances in public.

There was no doubt about it, Marc was a local celebrity and he always attracted an entourage of admiring female fans who wanted a piece of the action. It did feel good to be in Marc's company even though I was nothing more than a sidekick; someone that would do errands for him, like passing out telephone numbers to wannabes looking for a little bit of exposure.

Honestly though, it was of little consequence to me as I did start to enjoy my new found confidence and was sure things could only get better. I was always excited about the road shows I went to with Marc on his Golden Oldies nights even though most of the night I did nothing more exciting than sit by his side and pass messages backwards and forwards to the groupies that danced around their handbags on the dance floor.

Marc was always very protective over his daytime job as he felt this would damage his credibility and female fan base, and so it was that for those closest to him never divulged his real persona.

He meant well though, and I considered myself all the more enriched for having known him and giving me the direction and confidence that all played a part in where I am today. Between Marc and Rod, I think they had probably played every practical joke going. I was privy to some of the master strokes they played on others which included Doctors and Nurses. How they were never caught is beyond belief. Photocopied letterheads from the magistrates' courts for none payment of traffic violations like parking tickets that were put on the car windscreens of Doctors cars, fake letters from the environmental department of the City Council for premises inspections in Funeral Directors parlours and love letters sent to funeral staff of made up nurses from the hospital which again were all part of Marc and Rod's constant strive for the ultimate send up.

All good things however come to an end, and I guess the working conditions under the tight reign of Mr McCann had become for me untenable. I was always respected as part of the team with Roy, Colin, Tony, Reg and Sheila and had a great deal of respect for them. I had laughs a plenty and many a practical joke played both ways, but I was an inheritance from Mr Compton and Mr McCann resented this and didn't exactly hide the fact.

I had made up my mind to leave. This decision became all the more difficult as the lads and Sheila didn't want me to go, and tried their best to assure me that Mr McCann was more bark than bite and despite his tyrannical ways would come to accept me in time. My decision had been made and I left with one weeks' notice. I knew my passion for the job would always be a part of me, but for now it was time for a break to do something else.

For a time I had lost my way trying out 'normal' jobs but never really content on the daily chore counting the endless minutes to the end of every day. I knew that I would never be content in the 'normal' world but just needed a period of adjustment and change to get my life back in order. Good fortune would have it that I did find employment in a timber yard that made roof trusses at a time when this country was going through a housing boom. It was piecework and the only motive being money. The work was gruelling coupled with massively long hours that took no prisoners (no one ever did less than 80 hours a week). This was to be lesson of extreme discipline, doggedness and belief in one's ability to push the boundaries of your physical and mental state. Tempers among the gang would usually spill over on a daily basis over the pettiest of things and would sometimes result in a physical confrontation. So why the attraction? As I had said before...MONEY, and a lot of it.

It gave me the platform to the start of the rest of my life; a house, car, holidays, two great sons whom I am very proud of and an expendable income for other luxuries even though years later I was to lose the lot through a failed marriage.

Once I had got the two bed house, Ford Escort and 2.2 kids I felt it was time to return to my first love - the funeral profession. I knew it wasn't going to be easy to get back in as I had said previously no one ever leaves, but I had been told by Marc and Rod whom I kept close contact with that there had been big changes in my old work place. Mr McCann had been relieved of his duties and been asked to resign. Sheila, Tony and Reg had retired around the same time. Don Reeves had gone to another Funeral Directors within the society up in Leicester, Roy had done the same in the Midlands, and Colin returned to Bus driving in the valleys.

So, there was a new brush, and this was now a different society, a much bigger company than before. I did try on a number of occasions without success to go back, but there were no positions available at that time. They did promise to keep my details on file and that if anything turned up, I would get a call.

Not dismayed at this, and the slight glimmer of hope that one day I would return, I decided to take a part time job in a family Funeral Directors not too far from where my main interest was. I did this in conjunction with a night time job I had at the time. My shift started at 7.00 p.m. and ended at 7.00 a.m. then home for a quick wash and shave and out for any driving/bearing jobs at the Undertakers.

The biggest drawback to this is that the funeral home also had a branch down in Gwent, and was from time to time a requirement to also go on funerals down there as well some 40 miles away. Needless to say I was always completely and utterly wasted by the time the night shift started again. I did pull this off for quite some time, but eventually decided that working part time for the Undertakers all day for a little over £ 6.50 was really not worth it.

People that are in the funeral profession are a breed apart. For the most part, those in the job don't do it for the money. The basic pay is notoriously low, and can only be enhanced by over and beyond the normal hours acceptable by most to earn a liveable wage. However, money is also important, and my realisation of this meant that working all day for £ 6.50 was no good for body or soul, even if I really did enjoy the company I kept within the funeral parlour. Reluctantly I gave this up and again decided to earn some serious money with a different roofing company.

16. A Question of Faith

Who can ever know what is around the next corner and would we change our ways if we knew?

I am so glad that I don't the answer to any of these, and I would hope that despite the mistakes we all make along the way, there is a forgiving presence outside of our understanding that will give us the answer and ultimate peace of soul beyond this earthly life.

Whatever faith someone follows, should suffice for that person, and should not be judged by any other. I am not sure about Heaven and Hell; even Vicars couldn't give an honest account of it through personal experiences. As a Vicar once said to me of a question set by one of his parishioners in regard to what Heaven must be like. His reply was simply 'I don't know – I have never been there'. I appreciated his honesty. He furthered this by saying; he'd imagined it would be like whatever you thought it to be. We all have a passion about something or another and if sport was your thing then why shouldn't Heaven be like your favourite Sports Ground like Lords or the Oval, if clothes shopping was a passion then who says it shouldn't be like a never ending avenue of retail shopping malls in the sky?

My conclusion to this is that Heaven is a state of mind, not necessarily a place and certainly not in our time frame of weeks months and years. I believe that we as human beings are individual and the time and place wherever the spiritual home is, is infinite; yet as individual as we all are – all seven billion of us here on earth at any one time, we are no more unique than the next grain of sand on an endless beach.

One very ordinary day at work, my Nan gave me a call and was audibly desperate and emotional. This was out of character for Nan as she was the matriarch of the family and very strong minded. Emotion didn't come as part of the package with Nan. She was typical of so many of her era that kept home and family together, looking after daily chores and finances. She was an incredible woman with very high moral fibre and didn't approve of things that went against the grain. Because of her stance, she was never going to be a lovable cuddly Nan, just solid and unwavering. Nan never really gave away anything more than a smile of approval if you were in favour or a look of disappointment if you weren't; between those moments she was just solid counsel whether you wanted to hear it or not. So for the first time in my life this was a Nan that I didn't recognise with all her emotions exposed. As she tearfully tried to explain to me what was happening I could sense that she was struggling to hold on to her composure.

There are times in everyone's life when you just wished you were somewhere else; times when you feel helplessly low and lost and I knew Nan was in a lot of emotional pain as she gave me her account of what was unfolding before her, Dad and my youngest brother Mike. All I could hear was a lot of background anxiety and panic, but could also just make out voices of people that were very obviously paramedics or Doctors as they were reassuring everyone that they were doing all they could. At this point my whole world started to cave in and felt as if I was being swallowed by a huge void enveloped in a straight jacket, suffocating and feeling utterly useless. I think Nan hoped that by calling me I might have some miracle words of wisdom that would make everything right again; but I didn't. I was just as empty and useless as she and nothing I could say would change this.

Just then, a moment that seemed to last forever, Nan sobbed pitifully *'She's gone'*.

I put the phone down as the feeling of total sickness gripped in the pit of my stomach with vice like cramp.

'What's wrong?' someone said. *'My Mum's just died'* I said staring into space numb with shock.

Mum was 48 years old, leaving behind Dad, myself and my three other brothers Charlie, Joe and Mike who was 10 at the time and had witnessed the whole ordeal. She was also a Nan to my son Daniel. Mum was an only child and survived by Nan and Granddad. I have no doubt Mum was an Angel as she had the patience and tolerance and kindness of what I imagine one would have, but I so wished that she would have stood her corner and disagreed with others from time to time rather than accept whatever anyone else said. I don't think this world was ready for Mum and she certainly deserved so much more.

The bitter pains of death. There is no pain like it, yet as inevitable as it is, nothing will ever prepare you for it; we are simply not ready for it, not ever! In this Country alone there are around ¾ million people each year that die; you would think that as evolved as we are, we might have by now somehow been able to combat the feeling of loss.

I arranged the funeral with Dad as he said that I knew all about that stuff and would know what to do. Believe me, when things are that personal and close to home, you lose all comprehension of reality and everything seems so unnatural. I recognised all the forms before me and yet on this occasion it may as well have been written in French.

I kind of wished that just for that moment I had listened to Dad all those years ago and become a farm hand or lorry driver, but I wasn't and now I had to deal with the double edged sword of what I had done for a living and deal with mortality on a very personal level.

The Funeral Directors had undergone a major shakeup in staff and this was my first time back there since then.

The Funeral Director that helped us through the arrangements was a Mr Timothy Birch but was quite insistent we call him Tim, (now that would never have been tolerated in the old society).

Tim was of slight build and reminiscent of a young Charlie Chaplin to a tee minus the cane and flat feet. He was absolutely first class and guided us through the paperwork with relative ease helping us make difficult decisions. Tim played an enormous part in where I am today, thanks to his total care and respect to others and one for whom I will be eternally grateful to.

The day of Mum's funeral came but to be honest I cannot remember anything about it. I couldn't even tell you who was there. Selfishly I could only cope with my own thoughts and everything around me was inconsequential. Even though I had worked in the profession, I knew one day I would have to deal with this.

As I stared down into the jaws of this open grave sobbing uncontrollably, I now had a full understanding of grief and bereavement and I didn't like it one bit. Everything about it felt wrong and I felt cheated for all the things I could have said and done before her sudden and untimely death.

Certain things have happened in my life that I have no answer for. At these junctures in my life I have never sought any divination and it has always happened when I least expected it to.

What happened next can only be described as 'heavenly'. While back at work a few days later and unaware of any other thoughts other than the timbers I was preparing in the yard outside, quite unsolicited everything around me seemed to freeze in still mode. Just for a moment I wondered what on earth was going on. I could see fine, but my hearing was muted, when the most spiritually uplifting presence filled me and a voice I knew was Mums told me that she was alright. I looked around to see if anyone else could hear this, but everything was still on a different time frame. I got a little freaked by this, and thought I was going mad for sure, but then the calming reassurance of her voice came again *'tell the rest of them, I'm alright and that I will always love them'*.

I didn't think I had lost the plot, and consider myself of normal character. I have no reason to lie, but knew this sort of divine message passed on to the rest of the family at this time would surely book me a one way ticket to the funny farm, and so I chose not to. For me it was peace of mind, that all the things I never got chance to say or do, didn't matter as she knew all along. It didn't matter what path I chose in life or what decisions I made, as I knew somehow she was looking out for me. I cannot begin to find the right words to express what it feels like to have peace of mind but it certainly lifted a very heavy weight off my shoulders. My loss was still painful but at least for the first time I knew Mum was in a safe place and that she was alright.

Granddad doted on Mum and could never do enough for any of us; he was a real Gentleman, and I will never be able to find fault with anything he ever did. Sadly Granddad never recovered from the needless death of Mum and the loss only quickened his already advancing cancer which took his life three months later. He died at home with all his family around him and was buried next to Mum. I hadn't come close to going through a single day without mourning the death of Mum when Granddad died and I didn't fare any different this time. Even though I knew Mum was safe and Granddad had now joined her, it still hurt not having her around and my own selfish grief was more painful than I would ever let on.

I wasn't really surrounded by the right people that had any understanding of empathy at that time and for a while was all over the place with my own emotional state.

A call from out of the blue came shortly after Granddads funeral from Tim Birch the Funeral Director who had looked after us with Mum and Granddad. He had said that he didn't really quite know how to ask me considering all that I had gone through but that there was now an opening for me to come back to the firm. Naturally the timing was awful and he appreciated the fact that I may not be ready for a return so soon after both funerals. I thanked him for the offer and respectfully asked if he would give me some time to get my head around it. Of course the gentleman he was, he naturally said yes. I had deliberated all week after this not knowing if this was still really me.

I reflected on my divine message from Mum and waited for an approval that would say it was okay. It never came, but there again, it didn't need to. I remembered that it really didn't matter what path I chose as I knew Mum would always be looking out for me and so the decision was made for me there and then, and I called Tim to say that if the position was still there, I would be more than happy to return.

Not too long after I returned to the funeral business and this time more grown up and mature, another blow came to our family as Nan had been diagnosed with liver cancer. I wasn't sure how much more I could take of bereavement in my own family, but this time it was different. I know Mum was proud of me for who I was and what I did, but I did question myself why? Why was I chosen to do this? I had never looked for it and it had caused me nothing problems outside of work life.

I had wondered if I had made the right decision to go back and reflected on what we had all gone through in the last year. In the quiet of the early morning hours just before sunrise I took a walk for some fresh air. It wasn't something I did normally but for whatever reason I needed to clear my head. I was still none the wiser for where my fate lay when the soft uplifting voice of Mum came to me again *'don't leave, you'll be alright'*. This was to be the last time I would ever hear her voice again.

I know I am not mad, but I also know that in the bigger picture there is more to just what we can see. I cannot believe for one moment that at an undisclosed time and place we should be snuffed out like a candle. Whether religious or not doesn't matter. We all share a common element and that is we all live and breathe and what we do in this life must have a purpose to allow the next generation to evolve further otherwise there would be no point in being created in the first place.

I didn't leave, and yes I was alright even if I did now start to feel a little vulnerable advancing my position up the family tree.

As with Granddad, Nan also died at home with her family around her, and we had now lost all three within the year. Nan's funeral replicated Granddads and Mums before that with the same hymns and readings. It was now getting to be a venue for family get togethers and even the vicar was somewhat at a loss of words as to this series of deaths within our family over the last year and concluded in saying that *'I can understand if you would blame God in all this'*. Strange words from a man of the cloth I thought. I never gave it a second thought, and certainly didn't blame God in any of it. I was all the more enriched by Mum's messages I received after her death even if people would dismiss this as nothing more than a figment of my wishful imagination.

I didn't understand why at the time, but realised how truly privileged and blessed I was to know that this wasn't an end and was at peace that all three were now reunited, and for me that was alright.

So for me about the question of faith? Yes I do. It may not be the same as yours; but it doesn't matter. What matters is that you believe something. As for the vicar, well he will need to question his own faith.

17. And now for something completely different

I was back to my first love; working in the Funeral Directors that I had previously. The parlour had relocated from its original site and the coffin shop, mortuary and chapel of rest were now all contained within the same building, a far better arrangement for all concerned. The old society grounds had been sold off for the construction of a housing estate. It was ironic that I had played a part in constructing the roofs for the houses that were built on the old site where I had once worked.

There was a complete change of staff from top to bottom too, the old society had been taken over by a bigger society within the group. This time I was an equal and was treated as one from the outset, a far cry from the old company and some of the Victorian ways that dominated then.

Tim took a shine to me and taught me as much as he could which also gave me the platform to where I am today.

In no time he felt confident enough to encourage me to start arranging and directing funerals. It is one thing wanting to take the responsibility of such an important role but quite another actually fulfilling it. I had firsthand experience sitting on the other side of the table, and I knew what to do, but was I ready to take control and be the arranger? You can go through as many mock arrangements as you like, but actually sitting face to face with someone who has recently lost a loved one is something very different – I should know having recently gone through the same thing.

Naturally my first arrangement was not as fluent as I would have hoped; concentrating more on check boxes to make sure I had all the information rather than a relaxed flowing conversation. Tim was in no doubt of my sincerity and said that he was glad to have me as part of the team. Through his guidance he gave me as many opportunities as possible to arrange funerals as he said the only way I would get better would be to keep doing it. I was no longer the car cleaner or the general dog's body and tea boy. I had now moved into the middle ranks and I can't tell you how good that felt to feel that important. In time, the arranging became easier as I learned to relax more with families and have conversations rather than just questions and answers. There is no rule book as to how you arrange a funeral, because every family have their own ideas and their requirements are different too.

While arranging a funeral for a family one day, the topic drifted onto Victorian funerals and how things used to be. The family had said *'wouldn't it be good if they still had horse drawn carriages?' 'Yes I guess it would'* I said realising all of a sudden I was starting to get out of my depth. I knew what was coming. They then said *'could you get one?'* I had already anticipated that inevitable question before they even uttered the words. *'I don't know, but if it's possible then I will get one'*. I completed the arrangement and as we said our goodbyes promised I would look into horse drawns to see what I could do.

Tim was more than impressed with the way that I handled the arrangement especially as he knew that I had no idea whether there were horse drawn carriages anymore. The family left more positive than when they came in and hopeful that I might be able to do something special for them as well. Tim had said that he couldn't remember ever conducting a horse drawn funeral service and come to think of it he didn't know anyone else locally in recent times that had done one either. *'Well'* he said *'you've got your work cut out there then'* and gave me a load of directories to look through in the hope there might be someone that provided this type of service. It turned out that I found one such carriage master in Hertfordshire, who also said that he couldn't remember ever coming to this neck of the woods, but was more than happy to help. He gave me his charges and said to call as soon as possible if we still wanted him. I called the family immediately to let them know but that the carriage masters were from away and that the charge was quite expensive to come the hundred or so miles here. I could tell by the pause in conversation that the charge was obviously a concern, but undeterred the answer came back that *'yes, why not'* to which I replied *'leave the rest to me'*.

Tim was over the moon with the arrangements I had made, and promptly notified head office. The day of the funeral came, and the carriage masters arrived in plenty of time to groom the two Belgian Blacks and a final polish over the Marston Carriage. Naturally this attracted a lot of media attention as well as lots of onlookers and excited children that had probably never seen a horse close up. Unexpectedly the Regional manager Mr Rossiter from head office turned up and decided that he should take charge of the PR side of things and was in his element with lots of photos being taken particularly as the backdrop had the society name in it. Never to miss an opportunity he ordered Tim that he should hand out business cards to anyone that showed interest. It all started to turn into a bit of a commercial spin and I began to wonder what I got myself into. As we were about to set off the carriage master said to me *'where you going then?' 'In the hearse I suppose'* I said, not sure of the etiquette? *'Well, you can jump up here and ride shotgun if you want'.* Not sure whether this was right, I gratefully accepted as we followed the flower hearse to the house. As the horses trotted down the road, it drew more and more attention from people all around. To be honest, as special as it was, I felt exposed on the bench seat of the carriage riding 7 feet high and was now wishing I had opted for the less conspicuous enclosure of the hearse. The family had said that it had exceeded their expectations and thanked me for everything I had made possible. I didn't get so much as a bye or leave from the regional manager and I imagine he probably didn't even know my name as he constantly referred to me as 'mate' which of course I was not! Scores of business cards were handed out along the way and despite the company trying to cash in on the publicity, I was proud to say that I was the one that kick started an avalanche of horse drawn carriage funerals thereafter. Many people in the months that followed called to ask if it was our company that carried out the horse drawn funerals, to which we said it was. Of course we didn't, I had just hired the horses, but the general public didn't know that, and so it was that the company exploited the exposure of the event and still continue to provide this service today.

I never did get any recognition for my efforts, head office doesn't remember names, just results, but I was okay with that.

Today, horse drawn carriages are common place, and the sparkle has been slightly dimmed, but it was just the start of my thirst to explore other personalised requests that hadn't been done in recent times.

18. A very public affair

In the early hours of one morning, I had a call to attend a house in one of the more affluent areas of town. After taking down all the particulars I needed confirming name, date of birth, address, GP's details etc. Richard and I made our way there. The lady that briefed me with the information was the personal Nurse that had been employed in the house for some time and was very precise in her instruction making it very clear that we should not disclose the death of Sir Robert Cherrington to anyone. A strange request at 5.00 am in the morning, and it isn't something we do anyway. I gave her my assurance and said we would be there within the hour. En route to the address the 5.30 news came on announcing the death of Sir Robert Cherrington who died peacefully at home. So much for not disclosing any information I thought. It seemed that the radio station had been tipped off before we had even been contacted.

I have the advantage in not really following any current affairs or knowing any public figures, which thanks to my ignorance, means I never have any preconceived ideas about anyone. I treat everyone the same – rich or poor, famous or not. We all share the same common denominator, and I believe I treat everyone the same. On entering the house, the matron who greeted us had said that there was nothing for us to do and that Sir Robert had been already dressed in his funeral suit so there would be no need for any hygienic treatment from ourselves. She took great pride in letting us know this, and I was grateful that she had taken the time to do this. As she led us to where Sir Robert was, I couldn't help but notice that this man had obviously done a lot in his time for the town as there were framed letters prominently placed in a gallery style along the hallway that had been signed by the then Prime Minister Margaret Thatcher and even the Queen thanking him personally for all his good works.

I had no dealings with the arrangement, as this was being dealt with by one of the other offices. The Funeral Director on this occasion was Eve. Eve is still a good friend of mine today and works for another company now, who I see from time to time when they require a limousine for hire.

It was soon common knowledge about the arrangements for Sir Robert and this was broadcast on the radio informing that because he knew so many people of the town, that it would be only right and fitting the funeral should take place when most people had finished work in the evening so that everyone who wanted to, could pay their last respects.

Initially I thought this was possibly a little OTT, but then I didn't have any knowledge to what Sir Robert had achieved in the town. It was well known by now, that we had provided horse and carriage funerals for some time and again this was a request that Sir Robert should be taken on a set route through town taking in the Council offices where all the dignitaries would line up and then eventually onto the Church for the evening service.

Everything was perfectly organised, and credit to Eve for the hard work in arranging it all. Because of the enormity of the service Eve had requested another Funeral Director to co direct with her and asked if I would like to be one of the six pall bearers to which I naturally accepted. I never really expected the hype to live up to the reality, but how wrong I was.

The carriage masters that by now were quite familiar with our towns arrived in plenty of time, but this was the first time that Eve had been part of one. The groom had said it would be good for her to ride with the carriage and suggested it might be an idea if she practiced getting on and off. This wouldn't normally be a problem, but as it was expected to attract a lot of media attention, the last thing you would want is to get your footing totally wrong and fall.

It was just as well Eve did practice the mount as her pinstriped skirt didn't allow the give to climb the first step without raising it slightly which caused much raised laughter for her and all of us. The rather un lady like mount to the first step embarrassingly exposed more than it should of and the offer of a helping hand to the second step just seemed totally inappropriate. Eve did get the hang of it after a couple of goes, and laughed as she said *'well I suppose you all know now I don't wear tights'.*

As we left the funeral parlour and entered from the top of the town, the crowds lining the streets were starting to gather. A little further down where the dignitaries were already on parade more gathered, and on the final stretch through the town to the church the crowds were in their thousands. On this occasion myself and the five other bearers were to act as footmen, three each side of the carriage. I was wrong about my assumption of OTT; there were even television crews from all of the local networks filming for the evening news. On occasions like this, when you know the spotlight is on you, you become conscience of the fact that everyone else is looking at you. Don't get me wrong, it is a privilege to be part of something big, but it is also quite overwhelming and you do feel as if you're in a fishbowl. We arrived at the church in good time and entered the Church exactly on the hour. Once we had carried Sir Robert in we then waited outside until the end of the service as there was no spare seating available inside. The funeral was text book and we all congratulated each other afterwards on a first class performance.

Head office had different ideas though, and after playing the video tape backwards and forwards a few times came down to give their review on the proceedings as they saw it.

We were all called into our managers' office one at a time. Tim had naturally given his seat to Mr Rossiter and took his place to the side. Mr Rossiter was not someone to try and make idle chat with, he simply wouldn't wear it. The man had so much confidence about him you could almost mistake this for arrogance as he clearly thought he was a mile and a half above the rest of us and always took great delight in belittling anyone's efforts. Mr Rossiter was only a short man and of average build and wore bottle top glasses that magnified his pigeon eyes leaving you less than comfortable whenever he made eye contact with you. He would always put his glare to good use and had obviously practised this a lot over the years just to make you feel awkward in his company. Whenever he was around, you just made yourself busy as you could be sure he would find fault in something – that was his job.

His philosophy on the workplace was that to get the best out of your staff, you must insert unrest and encourage certain staff to stir things up from time to time to keep everyone on their toes. In this way, the higher management assumed you would maximise efficiency where no one could trust anyone. Tim wasn't that type of manager; he was a proper boss, a real gentleman that always got the best out of others because he would never ask anyone to do something unless he was prepared to do it himself. Because of Tim's approach to management he was never going to completely fit in at the top and I for one was deeply saddened when he left.

As I entered the office for my appraisal, Mr Rossiter was already comfortably seated, tilted back to the maximum of what the chair would allow, elbows planted firmly on the arms, fingertips touching, and looking down the bridge of his nose with his arrogant look of 'I am the Boss'. I could never work out how someone so short could always give the optical illusion of looking down his nose at you even when he was sat down. *'Well, how do you think you did?'* he said smugly. *'Very well, I think Mr Rossiter'* expecting this to be the safe answer. *'Not quite'* he bounced back. I felt he'd have had an answer for whatever I had said, so it really didn't matter what my reply was. *'Did you really have to look so serious like you belonged to the fucking Mafia?'* I couldn't answer this even though I had some choice thoughts, stunned that the Regional Manager had resorted to this lower level of appraisal. Tim cringed and felt as awkward as I. Thankfully this was his only criticism of me; I mean what did he want me to do? Wave at the cameras as I walked passed. I don't think anyone walked away with any positive comments even though we all knew it went like clockwork.

19. I felt like the exercise anyway

Those of a certain era that can remember the age of the Ford Granada will remember that cars were not as reliable as they are today. If the engine turned over you had a half a chance and if there was a morning dew, it probably wouldn't start at all.

You would think that hearses and limousines costing as much as they do and being garaged and well looked after would be saved the embarrassment of letting you down, but it just went to prove that cars back then were as reliable as the British weather regardless of maintenance.

One of your worst nightmares is a vehicle letting you down, and typical of any Funeral Directors you always have a pre armed list of excuses that hopefully would be plausible for any breakdown.

One autumn morning, we had a service to carry out some 15 miles away in a small village along the banks of the river Severn. Naturally the mist and dew was always denser as you got closer to the river, and this morning was no different. There is freshness about autumn that I like, and the mist that rolled off the river had a crispness that cleared your lungs.

The downside is that when the autumn leaves start to fall it can sometimes be hazardous when walking on them particularly if you have a coffin on your shoulders.

As we approached the village from the bottom of the hill, the Director then paged the hearse the short distance to the waiting family's house on the main road. Bob Thornton was the Director today from one of the satellite offices in the Forest. Bob was a Forester through and through with typical dialect that folk from this area have. He would refer to a hearse as hurst and a funeral to you and I was funrul to him but we all knew what he meant. It was always a standing joke with Bob as to how far he would page the hearse as he didn't like walking too far. We would often take bets as to how many steps he would make before getting back in the hearse, (this usually varied between 10 and 20 paces). No money was exchanged but the losing wager would usually be a forfeit of making the cups of tea back at base.

Bob was local to the surrounding villages and like in all rural areas everybody knows everyone else, and so it was on this occasion. Funerals out in the sticks are always different to town funerals. Time plays far less importance and everything is much less formal. Everyone is on first names and there was a good chance you would probably have been related to at least one or two people in the congregation.

As Bob walked to the front door to gather the mourners we as always stood to attention flanking the hearse. The principal mourners told Bob that they were still waiting for some family members to arrive. This posed no problem at all as the Church was only a couple of hundred yards away at the top of the hill. As we had to wait for the rest of the family to arrive, Bob signalled me to turn the engine off, so as not to look too eager. The plan for today was that the mourners would assemble behind the hearse and follow on behind at walking pace.

Patiently we waited and waited, until eventually the last of the mourners arrived. By this time I could feel my feet starting to go numb from the cold road and even the damp mist started to settle on our thick overcoats. Bob had naturally assured everyone that we were alright for time but that if they were ready we could make a start.

Thank Goodness for that we all thought. I jumped back into the hearse and turned the key only to hear a solitary click and then nothing. This is one of those moments when your heart just sinks. There is nothing you can do about it apart from look calm and in control when really you are panicking like mad inside. Okay I thought, turn off, key out and start again....click; nothing again. You know at this stage that everyone will be anxiously looking at you. I tried once again, but nothing. Quietly I whispered to Bob that it wouldn't start. Quite often in this job, you have to think quick and improvise the best way you can without anyone being any the wiser. Bob was a master of excuses; he had after all spent a lifetime doing this.

On this occasion he simply put it to the family that as we were so close to the Church, wouldn't it be nice if our bearers carried the coffin to Church. That may not sound too convincing but under the circumstances and faced with the predicament in hand, was actually a master stroke, especially when the family embraced the idea.

The coffin wasn't particularly heavy, but we did have to walk a couple of hundred yards uphill on a damp leafy uneven path. As experienced as we were as a team that worked well together, the incline halfway up the hill was now taking its toll on us and we were now visibly starting to flag. The Church was at least in clear sight but didn't seem to get any closer.

It was good that the mourners behind carried on chatting as if this was the way that we had always intended to conduct the funeral, totally oblivious to our now laboured efforts as the muscles in our legs were now starting to burn. Eventually we reached the peak to where the Vicar was waiting somewhat bemused as to why we had chosen to leave the hearse at the bottom of the hill. As we approached the Church I had said to Bob under my breath, *'don't stop now'* and he instructed the vicar to about turn and do the same. At this point I wasn't sure if it was sweat or mist dripping off my brows. Either way, we had certainly earned our crust for the day, and Bob had broken a personal record by walking more the 20 paces. As timings go, it could not have been more perfect. As we walked under the lych-gate and into the Church, the bell chimed in the hour and we were all justifiably proud of our achievement. Bob naturally wasn't best pleased as he had not walked that far in years and consoled himself with a well earned fag.

I am only too grateful on this occasion that the Church had their own trestles; otherwise we would all have collapsed on the chancel step with a coffin on top of us.

Of course on my return to the hearse quite predictably as I turned the key the hearse started first time.

20. Just making a point

From time to time we are involved with funerals of ex service men and women and when requested the Royal British Legion send representatives and even Standard Bearers from the local branch.

Even when ex service men and women are entitled to a Legion send off not all families want it, but for those that do, it is common place to expect One or more Standard Bearers, a compliment of members to form a guard of honour, the chairman of the branch will also read the homage in the service, and there would usually be the presence of a bugler to play the Last Post and Reveille. To compliment this it would be appropriate but not a necessity to have the coffin draped with the Union Flag or other ensign depending on who they served with, and a Poppy wreath from the Royal British Legion. On occasions it might also be wished that their beret and medals on a cushion are also placed on the coffin.

On this day we were to have the full works. All funerals are equally important and attention to detail is the same whether simple or elaborate. Naturally the more work that is involved the more you need to keep your staff informed of what is expected.

As days for a funeral can go, this was a particularly beautiful one; the crispness of a fine spring morning as the sun burnt its way through the early morning cloud almost guaranteed a pleasant day ahead.

The preparations were complete and last minute checks to detail were made. Indeed the coffin was draped with the Union Flag and an accompanying Poppy wreath and double ended lily spray from the widow placed on top of this. I am never keen on floral tributes on top of the Union Flag as etiquette says it shouldn't, plus the fact they can be prone to sliding off if not properly secured.

When we arrived at the church, we were received at the lych-gate by the waiting vicar and legion members. The family were told to hold on and chat amongst themselves while a couple of last minute checks were made inside the chapel just to make sure if the church had their own trestles or whether we needed ours. Although this has never happened to me, I do know on more than one occasion this has happened to other funeral directors where they had assumed the church had their own trestles only to find out that while processing down the aisle, one of the funeral directors worst nightmares (and believe me there are hundreds) becomes a horrible sinking reality of how on earth do I get out of this one? Of course they don't – they just make the best of a bad situation and quickly go back to the hearse to get their own trestles while the bearers are stood hopelessly waiting on the chancel step with a coffin on their shoulders.

No one is infallible and to human is to err; but we can certainly minimise those little hurdles that are also otherwise known as 'cock-ups'. It's all down to preparation, and the more you do this, the fewer things can go wrong – in theory anyway. Funerals in the main go without any hitch and it can be the easiest job in the world, but get something wrong and you can look totally inadequate and unprofessional. Of course, there is nothing you can do other than be able to improvise and think quickly on your feet when events out of your control happen. The secret here is to look totally unnerved by what calamity that is unfolding and have an outwardly exposure of calmness and control while inside the adrenaline rush feels like you're going to burst a gasket. As years go by this is a quality that all good funeral directors perfect as second nature.

Everything was now in place and we were all gathered at the lych-gate to proceed into church. The vicar led followed by the standard bearer, then the funeral director, the four bearers carrying the coffin and finally all of the mourners behind them in the usual form of nearest, dearest and everyone else. As we made our way up the path toward the waiting guard of honour, the only sound heard was that of the pea gravel underfoot.

For all the right reasons I will always remember this funeral, as it was an occasion when you just didn't see that one coming.

As the vicar led into church through the guard of honour, the standard bearer naturally lowered his flag to go through the same low entrance. I can only assume he must have thought he'd cleared the door, as he then mightily thrust the standard back into the upright position only for the brass point to embed itself in-between the overhead stone joist. We were no more than a few steps behind the funeral director and he just a couple of steps behind the standard and was aware very quickly what he had done. No matter how desperately hard the standard bearer tried to pull out the flag, it was jammed solid. Naturally refraining from laughter at such a comical moment we tried in vain to halt. Regrettably, the mourners behind were unaware of what was unfolding ahead and the swell of movement behind carried us on in a forward motion. I felt desperately sorry for the standard bearer as he patriotically held on to the standard and would not let go of it for love nor money. Regrettably we couldn't stop and bumped into the back of him. The way he fell to the floor you'd have thought he had learnt it at stage school as he stumbled and dived to the floor. The mourners were all in tears of laughter and I think even the vicar couldn't resist a titter while kneeling down to ask if he was alright. Of course he was, even if his pride was severely bruised, and I am sure even he laughed about it after. Incredibly he still had hold of the standard even when he was on the floor. Now that's what I call dedication.

> *They shall grow not old,*
> *As we that are left grow old.*
> *Age shall not weary them'*
> *Nor the years condemn.*
> *At the going down of the sun,*
> *And in the morning.*
> *We will remember them.*
> ***We will remember them.***

21. Trust me

I take my top hat off to all the grave diggers out there, that come rain or shine are out there doing a thankless job that is extremely hard graft. I have been down in a grave before now helping out and it is not the place for someone who suffers from claustrophobia. Grave diggers also have to contend with all sorts of soil conditions and put up with our very unpredictable British weather. Sometimes the ground is layer after layer of rock and stone and might only be possible to dig to a single depth. If the soil is very sandy, there stands a great chance of the sides collapsing, which is why you see so many that are shored up to prevent this happening. If there has been a lot of rain the grave can often fill up with water, particularly if there is a low water table or water course nearby. Grave diggers will dig what they call a sump which is a small hole at the one end of the grave to collect excess water. Sometimes, more often than not, this will not be enough and a pump is kept on hand for a last minute bail out before the congregation gather at the graveside.

Regrettably there is nothing you can do about nature, and if the rains keep a coming, then the grave will fill up. Grave diggers usually put a layer of cuttings or leaves over the surface water to disguise it as the last thing you want to see is a coffin bobbing up and down like a water buoy.

In rural areas, burials are more commonplace as it is a way of country life, though even this trend is now reversing. Cremations are more the norm in built up areas in suburbs, towns and cities.

It takes a special person to do this job, I mean let's face it; it is physically hard work, potentially dangerous, claustrophobic and if you're reopening a grave, you know that you're not the only one in there. When you have gone to the back busting lengths to dig the grave in the first place, after a short reprieve you then have to fill it all back in again.

Grave diggers are also a breed unto their own and are generally great characters. One such grave digger was Dangerous Dave. He was a great guy, and if you gave him a flask of tea and a pack of sandwiches would slave away all day like a true Trojan. Unfortunately, not the brightest biscuit in the barrel and also with not being able to read, didn't favour him too well as a contender for the Krypton Factor.

I liked Dave; he was a good hard worker that never complained. To look at Dave, you wouldn't think he could possibly do what he did for a living as his slight frame suggested he was in need of some body building steroids to cope with the manual labours of grave digging. With an expression of vacancy and glazed big brown puppy dog eyes you knew that you were never going to engage in any sort of sensible conversation with him. As a simple man he was easily pleased and was only too happy to be among company, even if he was taken advantage of by Phil his co worker and supervisor.

On one such day, Phil who usually managed to shy away from the physical duties of digging said to Dangerous that he had to deliver some paperwork to the local council offices and as it was urgent would need to leave him alone to dig the grave until he got back. Now Dangerous wasn't the sharpest pin in the cushion, but nor was he a total plank and second guessed that Phil was probably pulling a flanker. He gave Phil a look of disbelief and the tap of his index finger against the side of his nose and wink of his glazed eye as if to acknowledge this was priceless. *'No worries Phil leave this one to me'* he said assuring Phil he had things under control. *'Are you sure you'll be alright Dangerous – do you want me to mark the grave out?' 'Trust me'* came back the answer. *'Well alright, but if you get stuck, just use the template. 'Trust me'* again came the answer now just eager to get on with his job.

Phil drove off in his Ford transit van and Dangerous carried on about his work. Phil had a knack of always returning just at the right time to avoid any physical work. On this occasion, Phil hadn't paid too much attention to time and realised by his watch that he had been gone the best part of the day. He knew though that if Dangerous had a problem, he would have called him, so for what it was worth, everything should be okay.

Phil hurried back to the grave already armed with the excuse of something wasn't right with the paperwork which is why he was so long. As he looked over to the grave, he could see Dangerous sitting on the mound of freshly excavated earth crunching on one of the fallen apples, looking extremely pleased with himself at digging the grave totally unsupervised. *'Well, what do you think boss – didn't I tell you, you could trust me?'*

Phil was left speechless at what lay before him. *'Why the bloody hell didn't you use the template'* he said with total disbelief.

Dangerous was so enthused by the trust Phil had put in him, that he got just a little bit carried away with his measurements. You see, Dangerous was dyslexic and couldn't read a tape either, and so to be on the safe side had dug the grave ever so slightly larger.... larger to the tune of 9 feet by 4. (Most graves are dug up to 6 inches longer and wider than the actual coffin measurements).

Now on the verge of a panic attack, Phil said *'who did you think you were burying, the bloody Jolly Green Giant?'*

Dangerous laughed, and just didn't see what the fuss was about; far better to safe than sorry, he thought as he gazed blankly at Phil who was now beginning to go into meltdown.

In all fairness it was a bloody well dug grave, and Dangerous was proud of his achievement. Phil didn't favour so well with the council and had a lot of explaining to do.

Lesson: So the next time you think you are being clever in getting someone else to do your dirty work, and your co worker says *'Trust me'*, you might just be better off doing it yourself.

22. That's just grate

Pre 1980's the funeral profession as a whole was male dominated, apart from the handful of women Funeral Directors that were few and far between. Eve was an accomplished qualified Funeral Director and was, if you like one of the lads save the skirt, fishnet stockings and high heels, (what the lads got up to in their own time was none of my business). I had a lot of time for Eve, and she was also game for a laugh, but could also give as good as she received.

Although Eve was considered one of the lads, she was naturally all woman and I think she enjoyed the teasing she got about the fishnets. She would often play up her posh accent saying *'I wouldn't be seen dead in tights'* desperately trying to hold her composure without bursting into a fit of giggles.

Eve was a big hit with families with her modern approach and a breath of fresh air to the profession that was for too long stifled and unchanged by Victorian values.

She had been one of the co directors that made the funeral arrangements of Sir Robert Cherrington run so smoothly and I am sure that that funeral alone stamped her blueprint as a well respected Director within the profession.

Eve had her own branch within the company and naturally directed most of the funerals from there. Again after the usual run down of who, what and where we made our way to one of the high churches just on the outskirts of town. The church itself has a notoriously long walk which rises from the lych-gate to the church door and not for the feint hearted bearer should the coffin be heavier than normal.

Once Eve was happy everything was in place with the family and vicar she gave us the nod to carry on. Some vicars are oblivious to the perils that Pall Bearers undertake and can sometimes take a pitifully slow walk reciting chapter and verse without giving it a second thought that the bearers are actually carrying a coffin behind them. This was one of those vicars. Quite discretely under your breath, the bearers carrying on the front sometimes have to let the director in front know that the vicar needs to speed up a bit. The two bearers on the front also have to control the pace as the two behind may not necessarily see how close we are to running into the back of the Directors head – though this has been tempting at times is far better just to keep the image.

As we entered the church the vicar side stepped to the font and recited *'With this water we call to mind Ed's baptism....'.*

It is not unusual at this point for the vicar to sprinkle holy water over the coffin and at the same time spray the bearers' faces. I have seen a look of devilment in some vicars' when hosing down the coffin with their pastry brushes, as if by some chance it was accidental. The twinkle in the vicars' eye told you it was anything but.

The vicar turned again and carried on reciting as he led the congregation down the main aisle *'As Christ went through the deep waters of baptism for us, so may he bring us to the fullness of resurrection life with Ed and all the redeemed'.* He then continued with the opening sentences and stepped aside for the mourners to file into the pews.

One of the things that you notice with this church not untypical of a lot of others is that it has a tiled flooring with cast iron grating either side of the centre aisle, with the very old out dated heating system pipes visible just a couple of inches below.

As the vicar approached the chancel step to where the trestles were, he then branched off left to the pulpit reading from Proverbs 24 verse 16 '*for though a righteous man falls seven times, he rises again, but the wicked are brought down by calamity*' at the same time Eve branches right to allow us to place the coffin on the trestles, regrettably for her, her stiletto heel wedged tight in the iron grating. Off balance Eve quickly saved herself the embarrassment of falling, but in so doing snapped off her 3 inch high heel. Shaken by the predicament and not wanting to take her shoe off in view of everyone, made haste her exit hobbling like Long John Silver much to the amusement of all and sundry.

Outside the church, there was little that could be said to console Eve, so it was far easier as an icebreaker to just laugh about it.

The reading from the vicar could not have been more apt and Eve was for today now Jane - *'Calamity Jane'.*

23. Themes

I enjoy my job; not the inevitable death part that we all have to face, but the interaction with people that makes each day interesting and challenging. No two days or two funerals are ever the same. Even when the format is similar, we are taking care of individuals, and it is that, that makes each funeral unique.

By in large I think I have witnessed firsthand most conceivable events for a funeral, but no matter how many times it may be repeated it shows us how attitudes towards funerals have changed so much in the last 10 to 15 years.

Themes can play a significant part of a funeral requested by some families, and more and more people nowadays are not so afraid to express this. One such funeral I recall with fond memories was a themed service with the deceased wishes that all of the mourners should be attired accordingly in Blues Brothers fashion – smart suit, fedora hat and naturally, the sunglasses.

This was one occasion where we did know what to expect but when we arrived at the crematorium, it was quite clear that the family's wishes had not filtered through to all that were there, save the few immediate family that had taken the time to get their hats from a party shop in town. We were prepared for this big theme but were sadly disappointed to see that as the congregation lined up in procession to follow the bearers into the chapel, nobody bar the few had seemed to get into the spirit of things.

As we entered the chapel, the vicar paused to give the signal for the chapel attendant to start the music, and what other track could be more appropriate than 'The Blues Brothers' singing 'Everybody needs somebody'. As the music played to the signature tune scores of following mourners pulled from their pockets the sunglasses which looked absolutely brilliant. The timing was perfect and as an onlooker from a bearing perspective a real treat for us to witness; my only regret in hindsight was that I wished we had also worn glasses. I am sure the hairs on the back of everyone's necks stood up at this moment, me included as it truly was a memorable send off, one that I would definitely mark down as a favourite.

If there is anything good to come from a funeral then I think it is the memories you can take with you, and when families personalise things away from the norm, I am sure in time a lot of positives are drawn from it. The Blues Brothers theme was a real treat for everyone and one that will be remembered by the family forever I am sure.

Not everyone can cope with something so radical and sometimes want to be different but in a less elaborate way. I remember the first time I was asked if I could get a Highland Piper to play the Bagpipes as we entered the crematorium chapel.

Naturally I said if there was one, I would get one. Having read through my listings of musical alternatives, it just so happened a Highland Piper lived locally in the nearby town. His charge was £100.00 which seemed a bit steep considering it was the same price as one that would have travelled from Birmingham 50 miles away.

A piper will generally turn out in a number two uniform which is less formal than the number one and rather more contemporary.

The Number Two uniform has a kilt and is accompanied by an Argyll jacket, shirt and tie, ghillie brogues and a horsehair sporran.

The piper will wear knee high socks known as diced hose, of handmade, patterned Scottish wool. Tucked into the top of the sock will be the famous Skean Dhus, the small knife, (or dirk, to the Scots), which will usually feature a ruby in the handle as well as clan or Celtic designs. Often, flashes, in either the clan tartan or perhaps a plain colour, will be worn under the top of each sock and will provide an eye-catching contrast to the whiteness of the sock itself.

I always enjoy the experience of a first time for everything and this again was one of those moments. I had paged the hearse for the short distance to the entrance of the crematorium and introduced myself to the Piper who was attired exactly as described while the hearse followed the loop road around the back of the crematorium to eventually pull up under the canopy to where I was standing.

The Piper had simply said to give him the nod when I wanted him to start up; what could be simpler? Everyone knows what bagpipes sound like, we've all seen them on the Royal Variety Shows or Edinburgh Tattoo, so there are no hidden surprises and therefore I decided to take my place beside him. I had given the Vicar and bearers the signal to start and also the family that they should follow my bearers.

At this instruction I then discretely told the Piper to start whenever he was ready. As he filled the bladder with a couple of deep breaths he then released the first note.

What I wasn't expecting was for the first note to be so deafening. It visibly startled me and I damn near jumped out of my skin as my ear drums were slowly adjusting to the pitch. In one ear I had to put up with the constant ringing of tinnitus and the other the drone of the pipes. Needless to say, I never got caught out on that one ever again.

24. Time please

There are certain rules and regulations that we all have to adhere to when complying with the crematorium's requirements. As funeral directors we are held accountable for this i.e. what is permissible in the sense of whether the coffin material is compliant with the emissions that is released into the atmosphere from a cremation, also personal clothing that the deceased may be wearing, in particular it is generally noted that although family's may provide footwear, that they should be removed prior to cremation due to the synthetic fibres that they are made from; you can probably imagine what emission might be given off if Granny were still wearing her favourite slippers.

The crematoria have to be strict about this as the last thing anyone wants to see is black smoke filling the air with a burning rubber smell as it billowed from the top of the incinerator flu – honestly and truthfully, I have heard relatives say before now *'well, there goes Granny'*. That really can be an awkward conversation stopper, as there is no answer to that.

Of course there are other things to be aware of as well like, photos still in glass frames, big cuddly toys made from non compliant materials. I cannot count how many times that packets of cigarettes have been placed with the deceased which is not a problem, however you need to be vigilant and check all of the pockets to make sure that no lighters have been slipped in.

People have asked me on other occasions if they can place a bottle of whisky or Gin in the coffin as it was their favourite tipple. The simple answer is that if it is combustible then the answer is no; if it will give off an emission not compliant with the rules and regs then the answer is again no.

The cremators are highly detailed and sensitive pieces of equipment that are controlled by modern computer systems that enable the operator to know exactly what is placed in the coffin just by the emission it gives off. An emissions report of each cremation is logged and sent with all of the other cremation reports on a pro rata basis to the local municipal offices for the environment to observe that the crematorium is operating within the allowed guidelines for emissions. An environmental officer can deny a licence to cremate if this doesn't meet the criteria and so it is vital everyone knows the rules.

Working in this profession carries a two edged sword as you know there will be times when you are the one attending the funeral rather than directing it. When you arrange and direct funerals for others, you are always cross examining yourself as to whether you have covered everything you need to. In the same way you quite unconscientiously find yourself detailing the practices of others – almost marking their performance. I don't think this is a bad thing as I would be the first to admit I have picked up on good ideas from other funeral directors and adapted my own take on it, but also make sure that if I don't like something I see, that we don't do the same.

There is something very surreal when I attend funerals of people I knew as I can often remember conversations we had had, sometimes quite recently. The very fact that as a human race we have this rhetoric and physical interaction with our own kind, leaves me in no doubt that this is not the end. How can it be? We have for the most part evolved into a relatively intelligent species, and if it were all for nothing, then there would be no point in any of us even getting out of bed; but we do wake up every morning, some more purposeful than others, but wake up we do – how we choose to start the day and finish it is up to us. So whether it is by faith or a higher level of existence, I cannot accept that when our time comes, that's it as if we were never here.

I remembered well a neighbour that I would share pleasantries with each day. He would always greet me with his monotone catchphrase *'morning Jan, have you got the time?' 'Yes I do'* I would always reply and politely smile as I predictably also knew that his next line would be, *'looks like it's going to be a nice day today'*. It could have been raining cats and dogs and he would have said the same. This was a conversation he had with everyone, so at least I wasn't getting any preferential treatment there. It's funny that no matter how well or not you knew someone, that when they're gone no matter what their standing in life was, you will miss them. It took some time for me to get used to the fact that I wasn't going to see him again, as trying as he was at times, particularly when I was in a rush.

The bearers carried his coffin into the chapel, placed it on the catafalque, bowed, turned around and waited for all of the congregation to be seated before making their exit. As the vicar was just about to give her welcome, a digital alarm was heard coming from his coffin to signal the hour.

I held back my smile and thought about how many times in all the years I knew him, he had asked me the same question every morning, when all along he had his own watch. Of course the watch was removed before the cremation took place, much to the embarrassment of the funeral director concerned, and yes it was also a nice day!

25. Hey big spender

If I live to be 100 years old, I still don't think I will have seen everything in this business. You can assume so much, and in the main you will be right, but just when you thought you knew all there was to know, something totally out of the blue will happen that will make you smile from ear to ear.

As far as out of the ordinary goes, I don't think this funeral will ever be beaten. It wasn't comparable to anything I had ever seen before or seen since.

Our orders were the same as it always was and everyone knew what to expect. There were to be no hymns played at the service today; just CD's to come in and leave to. This has become more commonly requested over recent years, and believe it or not there is even a top ten chart, although today's track was most definitely not in that list.

We knew that there was likely to be a large congregation as the funeral was of a young man. Regrettably through no fault of ours but traffic delays with road works and 3 way traffic signals, we were running a little behind schedule.

Mobile phones were very much a new thing back then and were the size of house bricks, but thank goodness we had one in the hearse as we phoned ahead to let the crematorium know we were running late. The crematorium can at times seem like a bit of a sausage factory; as one goes in another comes out, and can also seem a little too commercial. When there are back to back services every half an hour, then the crematorium needs to be super efficient and to be fair the chapel attendants are exemplary in their duties.

Because of the then modern technology of the mobile phone, we were able to ask the chapel attendant to help us out by having everyone seated before we arrived which he did. By the time we were pulling up the crematorium drive there wasn't a soul in sight with everyone sat inside awaiting our grand entrance.

One of the most important things any funeral director must do on any funeral is never to look rushed. At all times we must show control even if we are having kittens inside and your stomach is turning ten to the dozen. The philosophy being that if you are running late, you are late and that's that. If you try rushing you lose dignity and professionalism; families need to know that time doesn't matter, even if it does.

When you have a good team working together as we did; when things get tight, you know you can all rely on each other and with military style precision each person knows what to do without saying anything. With the coffin on our shoulders and family behind us, the director signalled the chapel attendant to cue the music. As we walked down the centre aisle behind the vicar we were greeted by a congregation full of bright colourful floral dresses - not a sign of black anywhere, this true to form was in keeping with the family's request. The music played Shirley Bassey's 'Big Spender' as we entered the chapel which regrettably brought about the most embarrassing mincing from two of the bearers, one of which was carrying next to me.

As the CD of Shirley Bassey sung the opening line *'The minute you walked in the joint'* Niall who was carrying on the front with me and Simon who was on the back decided to swing their hips left and right to the tune. I almost died on the spot when they did this hoping no one had noticed for fear of a disciplinary and almost guaranteed dismissal when we got back to the office.

Just when you think it can't get any worse - it does. Panic and anxiety are camouflaged by contained nervous laughter as the music continues with Shirley singing

I could see you were a man of distinction, a real big spender

Then out of the corner of my eye I noticed that the whole congregation was full of every imaginable cross dresser going, some with handle bar moustaches. Somehow it just seemed too surreal to be a funeral and all of a sudden found myself struggling to keep control of all my bodily functions. The ordinarily short walk to the catafalque seemed to take forever with a feeling of one step forward and two back. I don't think I have ever gripped the inside of my cheeks with my teeth as hard in my life. Inside, my body was shaking nervously out of control, my ribs now aching with silent laughter and the beads of sweat that suddenly started to roll down my forehead as if I had just eaten a Phall curry. The song continued:

Good looking, so refined
Say, wouldn't you like to know
what's going on in my mind?

The coffin was eventually placed on the catafalque; we bowed and turned, waiting for the signal from the director to leave. Those few seconds seemed like a life time, as I tried so desperately to hold it together. I am in no way homophobic, but felt very uneasy about the whole ceremony and I am sure if I was aware of what had been planned, I could have prepared myself better. Niall and Simon did know what to expect as they had friends that were part of the congregation and knew what they could get away with.

We walked out much quicker than we came in to the last few lines

So let me get right to the point
I don't pop my cork for every man I see
Hey big spender!
Spend a little time with me.

Even Niall and Simon burst into tears of laughter as the chapel door was firmly closed behind us, and it took quite some time for me to regain my composure again before the end of the service. Surprises I can deal with but shock I can't. I can honestly say that I had for the first time experienced a mild form of shock.

I can also say that I never want to experience it again.

26. Harmonising

If I were ever envious of anyone, it wouldn't be of any one person but to people that have a natural talent that can genuinely sing in tune. I am sure we all from time to time sing out loudly in the bathroom thinking it to be a soundproofed haven for the tone deaf, but if truth had it; I would bet that 99.9% of us needn't bother auditioning for 'X Factor'.

John Stroud was one of our more senior driver bearers that was in his youth an accomplished choirboy with a reputedly good voice. In recent years however he had regrettably become profoundly deaf in both ears, and even with both aids on maximum volume still had to lip read best he could what was being said. I can't imagine how lonely his world had become particularly to someone who could once hear quite perfectly.

I liked John a hell of a lot and to be fair I have usually got on much better with people that are older than me. Not everyone gave John the time of day as they were as frustrated as he - for them not being able to make themselves understood and for John interpreting the wrong words. I felt quite sad for John, because he was a genuinely nice man that through no fault of his own was becoming isolated through his deafness.

For those of us that can't sing, (me included!), it can be quite painful sitting through a service when the vicar asks you to please stand and join me in singing……and then the only two voices you can hear is the vicar (who again will probably be as bad as you) and the organist (that thankfully usually can).

This didn't faze John, as he always proudly told everyone on more than one occasion that he was once a choirboy. Regrettably because John had become deaf in his latter years it was very difficult for him to adjust to his disability. Whenever we sat in the service to accompany the singing of hymns, it became difficult for the rest of us to sing when John was always at least a few words adrift. At times I would point my finger to the line that the rest of us were singing, which he acknowledged gratefully with a thumbs up. There were times when I don't think the organist knew whether to speed up the music or slow it down just to keep in tempo with John.

But it wasn't just the tempo, it was also the tune. A lot of hymns are relatively easy to sing and can be fairly monotone, but some have high and low notes together for example the hymn we all know as 'How great thou art!'. Unfortunately I have to admit that I would dread this hymn being played as John also tried to hit these high and low notes. As he obviously couldn't hear his own voice and could barely make out the tempo, this hymn was one of the most painful ones to attempt and sounded as bad as an alley cat being strangled. We had all at times tried to encourage John that he didn't need to sing, but we all knew that he loved to do it, and it seemed disrespectful to a man of his age to hurt his feelings, even if he did murder the singing.

The funeral today was in a picturesque town in the Cotswolds. It was in a Methodist Church which we had been to many times before. Unfortunately this Church has always caused us grief as the entrance door to the chapel turns a sharp left once you have come through the main door. Geometrically speaking it has always been a nightmare as you can imagine coffins don't bend around corners, and so the pall bearers have to do a lot of careful manoeuvring to get through. Once you had successfully negotiated this obstacle the side aisle was barely wide enough to safely carry the coffin without hitting the pews either side, denting a few hip bones on the way down.

If I didn't know John as well as I did, I would have sworn blind he had been working for 'Candid Camera' on this day. It was almost like something from a 'Chuckle Brothers' sketch. It was normal practice that as we entered through the first tight left corner that the one bearer on the front would slide around, still taking the weight so that the two of us could get through, and then the same would happen on the back end.

John had forgotten our normal routine and for reasons best known to him decided to stay where he was. The forward motion regrettably wedged both John and I in the door frame with the coffin still on our shoulders. Neither of us were particularly large, but wedged we were. The two bearers behind decided the only course of action was to push us through.

I suddenly knew what it felt like to be a champagne cork. The handles either side were now pressed tight against mine and John's cheekbones and I could feel the hard edge of the door frame digging into the side of my face. Just as I didn't think it could get any tighter; my cheeks now embedded into the door furniture, John grunted, and as he did one of his hearing aids sprang over the top of the coffin somersaulting perfectly to the floor. Now, it's fair to say, I consider myself a professional, but I really didn't know whether to laugh at how funny that was or cry for the pain inflicted by the door frame.

Eventually the coffin was in position and everyone was seated, us included. As we brushed ourselves off still recovering from the fiasco that John had put us through, the vicar announced the hymn we were all dreading 'How great thou art!' We were all accustomed to how out of tune John's singing had become and so expected no great shock that this would be anything different. Unfortunately no one had retrieved John's earpiece which made the organ music even harder for him to pick up on.

As the chorus played *'then sings my soul, my saviour God, to thee'* John carried on the note much longer than it needed. As he finished the note the congregation were already on the next line. John was now already three words behind and unaware of how loud he was singing causing a lot of unwanted attention from the rest of the congregation. I did manage to point out to him where we were singing from, so he was at least now on the same line. Unfortunately I couldn't stop him warbling his way through the next three verses and totally crucifying a relatively nice hymn.

Mobile phone cameras weren't the norm back then, but if they had, I imagine that sketch would have been worth a small mint on the small screen.

27. Full moon

Over the last thirty years I have seen four of the cottage hospitals in the County close. Two of the companies I had worked for had carried on from the porters day shift to the out of hours assistance that required our services for any night time duties; this was basically a service that the two of us on call would go along to the wards in any of the contract hospitals at the time to transfer the deceased from the wards to their private chapels of rest within the grounds of the hospital – this was usually from 8.00 p.m. to 7.00 a.m. before the day porters took over again.

When all of these hospitals were fully operational, night time duties could be quite busy and it wasn't unusual to find yourself out quite a lot of the night driving from one hospital to another and then sometimes back again before the dayshift came back on.

Creeping around in the early hours is not my idea of having fun, and I jump at things that go bump in the night the same as anyone else especially when you are minding your own business in tranquil thought and then the phone rings making you jump out of your skin for another callout.

Night duties always give you plenty of time to think, sometimes too much, and when your brain is relaxing in drift mode all sorts of noises are magnified. Your sense of hearing is far more acute when the daytime world has gone asleep. Any slight noise is exaggerated and the rustle in the undergrowth is usually nothing more than a hedgehog foraging for food. The mind is a powerful tool when there is nothing else to think about on the graveyard shift.

One such hospital contract we had was in the valleys where we would probably attend two, three sometimes more nights a week to do the transfers from the ward to their chapel. The hospital was set in acres of beautiful grounds in the countryside on the side of the hill with its own lake and landscaped gardens, lots of wildlife like wild deer, rabbits, badgers and peacocks and a breathtaking panoramic view across the county.

One clear night we had the call to attend the wards where it was normal procedure to first go to reception to get the key for the mortuary and receive confirmation of who and which ward we were to transfer from. Then we would attend the ward and again confirm with the Ward Sister who we were to transfer, carry out our duties by transferring the deceased patient onto our stretcher and then drive the short distance around the back of the hospital to the mortuary. Once inside the chapel it was simply a case of transferring the deceased patient from the stretcher into their cold room.

Regrettably the wind up trolley in their mortuary to place trays in and out of the refrigeration cabinet was so old it must have been antique. It was heavy and made of cast iron so naturally very cumbersome to wheel around. The wind up mechanism operated manually by a large crank handle and took so long to raise or lower, it was much quicker not to use it at all; but for the purposes of health and safety you always did, even if it did take forever.

Once the details had been logged into the register, there was nothing more to do other than lock up and take the key back. It was always quicker for me or the other person on call to quickly run around the side of the building to hand the key back into reception while the car made its way round.

This didn't bother me as I had done it so many times before at night and knew where every pot hole, divot and hedge was blindfolded. As I quickly made my way around the gravel path and onto the gardens I heard a noise that stopped me in my tracks. Momentarily, all my senses came to the fore as I scanned my limited vision to see what was there, but could see nothing; and so I took another step and again another rustled noise. Not sure what it was and certainly not wanting to find out I quickly hastened my way toward the reception light. As I did, an excruciating shriek came from under a bush that sounded like a wailing banshee. The sound deafened me and at the same time took about ten years off my life. I had disturbed one of the resident peacocks.

Totally alarmed and in defence mode its feathers fanned out making a shimmering noise as it identified me as a predator. At this point I was about two seconds away from a heart attack and can guarantee I was a hell of a lot more startled than the bloody peacock.

Still shaken by this, and the immediate panic of being attacked by something far more dangerous than a peacock now subsiding I swaggered my way back to reception. My on call colleague for some reason couldn't stop laughing at what had just happened. I on the other hand didn't think it was very funny at all.

I never stopped returning the key this way – just more observant where I was walking, after all, it was their habitat, not mine. The hospital closed down a few years ago due to more NHS cut backs, and I for one was very saddened by this, as I had been a patient there myself a couple of times and had nothing but praise for the place.

I have no idea what happened to the peacocks but trust they found new homes. When the hospital closed their doors for the last time they did send me a hardback copy on the history of it and personally thanked me in recognition of my services over the last 25 years.

28. Highly Infectious

It goes without saying that there are going to be times when you have to deal with the inevitable higher risk diseases like hepatitis, Tuberculosis (TB), Creutzfeldt–Jakob disease (CJD) – the list goes on, and it is imperative all staff are aware of any cases and that all precautions are adhered to for the public health and safety of others. As long you are sensible, there is no reason for undue concern.

Out of hours duties were supposed to be on a rota basis, but on account most of the lads preferred their social life usually ended with me taking on their shift. It didn't bother me as I was in need of the extra work anyway.

On this night I was on call with deaf John who I would pick up en route from his home. He had a special telecom system with red flashing lights and a speaker that enabled him to hear my voice whenever I called.

I had received a call to attend an address where the gentleman that had died had TB. I didn't know this until we were greeted at the door by the district nurse who had been part of the palliative care team looking after him in his last days.

John was always okay with me as he could lip read me easier than the rest of the staff as I used to accentuate my mouth movements so he stood a chance of what was going on. Obviously when you are in people's homes, you need to be careful how audible you are therefore you just got on with the task in hand with minimal speech. John was understanding of this and didn't feel the need to say anything as I was the mouth piece.

As we entered the room on our own where the deceased lay, I signed to John TB.

John was surprised that I had taken the time to let him know this, but I could see by the look of grateful acknowledgement that he was more than appreciative of my sign. He acknowledged this by giving me his usual thumbs up. I didn't really know how to sign and my limited knowledge was what I had picked up from him. Back en route to our premises John thanked me again and I could tell it meant a lot to him.

Not all cases are as simple as that. On another occasion my Manager asked me to go to the City hospital while on day duties to collect a body that had a high risk infection. I went on my own as no one else was keen on going, and I knew that I would get help the other end from Rod and Jimmy (the two mortuary technicians).

As I reversed into the turnout, Rod and Jimmy were already waiting for me and had been tipped off I was on my way. They were both still dressed in full PM gear fully togged from head to toe which I thought highly unusual at two in the afternoon as post mortems were usually completed by midday.

Rod and Jimmy were straight faced and unusually serious which was a side I had never seen in either of them before. Jimmy had replaced Marc who had left to further his career in media. Jimmy was the perfect replacement for Marc as he had the same mischievous manner. Today was different though, and I could tell that Rod was not joking as he briefed me on the body I had come to collect. He had asked me if I knew what I was dealing with, to which I confirmed I had no idea.

Rod and Jimmy led me into the bay where the body in question lay. As with all of the deceased they are individually sealed in body bags with labels for identification on the outside as well as the inside. Rod told me that he and Jimmy had on this occasion double bagged the body as a precautionary measure and advised me that I must not under any circumstance look inside because of the disease the person had died from.

I was obviously inquisitive about this as I had been around most causes of death and never had to be this careful before. Rod then took me into the changing room where he gave me the same attire as he so that I could safely complete the transfer from the mortuary back to base. I had known Rod for many years and he had spent most of these years playing practical jokes on anyone he could; but this time he was different – he didn't share his latest send up or lark around the way he always used to, he was just as cold as ice. *'So what is it then Rod?'* as I started to put on the apron, face shield, surgical gloves, over shoes and surgical cap; *'Lassa Fever'* he said quite seriously.

I said slightly unsure and not wanting to commit myself to looking a total idiot *'I had heard of it but had no idea what it was apart from it was a deadly virus from somewhere in Africa'.*

'You're not joking there' he said. I couldn't quite work out why there was a Lassa fever case here though, and so I started to smell a rat – *'Rod'* I said to him in a quietly

threatening voice as I stared him eye to eye *'if you're winding me up, I will personally come back and stick these gloves where the sun don't shine'. 'I wouldn't do that to you Jan, not this time'.* Somehow I wasn't convinced, until he said I should call the Manager back at base if I didn't believe him. That was good enough for me and as ridiculous as I looked – all dressed up for biological warfare, I loaded the stretcher, got back in the van and drove back to base.

The route back to base was a short one but one that had a level crossing whose barriers were usually down even when there were no trains in sight for anything up to ten minutes at a time. I had hoped that just this once they would stay up long enough for me to get through. As it was, I was starting to attract odd looks from pedestrians as I drove past, and as luck would have it – you guessed it, the barriers came down. At this point, I don't mind telling you I was starting to feel very uneasy about the looks I was getting as more and more people gathered at the barrier waiting for the train to pass. It was an uncomfortably baking hot day anyway, and with the extra aprons and over clothes I was now wearing I began sweating so profusely I may as well have had a hose pipe running water down my face. The sweat started running into my eyes which began to sting and made it difficult to see properly without removing the face shield which I had been categorically told to keep on. I was now beginning to wish I was anywhere but here stuck on a level crossing.

Eventually the barriers lifted, and it couldn't have happened soon enough as I was glad to be underway again. Base was only a half a mile down the road, and as I turned into the yard I was greeted by the entire workforce as they all universally clapped and cheered me in. The bastard I thought. I had been totally and utterly stitched up. I was too long in the tooth to have fallen for a simple practical joke, but this was well engineered on all fronts, and they had certainly got one over on me.

I was angrier at myself for not seeing that one coming, but acknowledged that it was at least a damn good prank, even if it was at my expense. Just to put the reader at ease, the body turned out to be none other than a resusi Anne that is used in first aid programs – the legs were some prosthetic limbs they had in the store room.

The next time I returned to the mortuary, Rod and Jimmy were all smiles and laughter; Rod looked slightly nervous as I had a pair of surgical gloves in my hand. The answer is no I didn't.

29. Ding Ding

One of the disadvantages big companies have is that the bigger they are the more complex the running day becomes as you have to carefully plan the movements and actions of all your staff. Invariably there is never enough staff to cope with events in a normal way which leaves the majority running around like headless chickens from one funeral to another.

Most of the driver bearers came from the head branch in the City where they were designated what funerals they were on and which branch they would leave from on their daily worksheet. Sometimes it was a necessity to run from one branch to another at short notice. Today was no different. I was already in one of the satellite branches awaiting Niall to come over and drive the hearse on ours. The news came through that Niall was behind schedule on the other funeral because of a delay at the crematorium from a previous service over running.

It goes without saying, that when you are minute watching desperate for your driver to turn up, it shatters your nerves as you start to impatiently pace the yard wishing that time would just stop.

The hearse was already loaded with a sea of flowers that surrounded the coffin inside and flowers that covered the top of the hearse too. Only right and proper that on this occasion where the funeral was of a bus driver who worked for the local coach company that the main floral tribute was of a big red double decker bus with a model conductor that stood beside a bus stop. The tribute was far too big to place in the hearse, so we opted to make it secure on top against the roof rails of the hearse.

I am never keen on flowers on top as they are open to the elements, but if they are secured tight enough, they are usually fine. Niall did eventually turn up through no fault of his own but we were still running desperately late. With no time to spare we were off and down the main A40 to get to the family's house. If there were no flowers on top, I wouldn't have given it a second thought for the necessity of picking up the pace we needed to reach the family, but when there are flowers on top, even when they are fastened, I still only like to keep to around 20 mph.

Sometimes everything just goes against you, and the signs were definitely not favouring us today. Just as we were on our way and pushing a steady 30 mph the lights changed very suddenly (they always do when you're in a rush). There was no way we could have driven through as it was already on amber and Niall had already pushed his luck previously on other traffic offences. As controlled as he could possibly be, Niall brought the hearse to a halt just edging over the line. At this point, we could hear the already forward sliding motion of the flowers along the rooftop vinyl toward the front screen. Fearing the worst that we were about to lose everything on top, thankfully the red double decker bus wedged under the front roof rail and stopped any others flying off. Regrettably though the conductor did come unstuck and tumbled over the rails bouncing off the bonnet and landing on the pavement right next to .....the bus stop.

It was a surreal moment as you couldn't have made that happen even if you had rehearsed it a hundred times before. Niall and I looked at each other speechless, momentarily stunned at the situation and hoping no one else had noticed. I quickly got out while the lights were on red, picked up the conductor and carried on as if nothing had happened. Just before we got to the house, and out of view, I replaced the conductor back in his rightful place and no one was any the wiser.

We did make up time, and everything went like clockwork no thanks to head office trying to make the impossible possible.

30. A change is as good as a rest.

An opening came about in 1996 for a manager position with another part of the society in the next County. It had come at a time when I was in need of a change. I was for the first time moving into the management structure and quite frankly I wasn't overly confident whether I was up to the task.

Managers come and go in big companies and the job security is less favourable than that of the driver bearers. You have targets to meet and if you don't; you need answers. Sometimes there are no answers, but that is an excuse that head office will never wear.

I had nothing to lose, and so with lots of good luck cards and well meant messages of support, I went. I was lucky enough to have a flat that went with the position, and so it was an exciting challenge all round that lay ahead. My Area Manager was absolutely brilliant and she gave me whatever support I needed. Just like my previous employers, the vehicles for funerals came from the main branch some

20 miles away, which wasn't ideal and I always had to make sure that they were not already committed to other services before I confirmed dates and times with my families.

My branch was a fairly small one in a town that used to conduct around 400 funerals a year until the previous owner sold out and one of his employees who lived locally at the time set up half a mile away and pretty much took the client base with him over night.

The numbers had been declining for some time and were now only conducting around 80 services a year. I won't lie and say that I turned this around, but I did get a taste of my first real baptism into management and the scrupulous practices that can go on.

My Area Manager had pretty much given me a free card to do as I wished to find out where the company was going wrong. The problem Head Office had and acknowledged was that without the right person based in the satellite office it was impossible to know what was going on. One of my first introductions was to make myself known to the registrar and the staff.

I was absolutely gobsmacked to learn that the company across the way provided free of charge town maps and how to get to their premises once they had registered the death. This practice is bang out of order and in my nicest possible way suggested to the registrar that we too should also have our name printed on the town maps. Head office thanked me for the news and agreed for me to go ahead and get printed some maps which I forwarded to the registrars. The Registrar slightly embarrassed apologised if the previous maps had diverted people away from our office and immediately placed the new town maps with both company names in the information racks for people to make their own informed decision.

I think the damage had already been done though, as the maps had been in the registrars for goodness knows how long, but at least I was able to steady the declining numbers for the time I was there.

There were a lot of farming communities around the town I now worked in and I was not the least bit surprised to be asked by one of the farming families that lived just on the outskirts of the town about a horse drawn. *'No problem at all'* I said, as I had now become quite a dab hand with these. The family were somewhat surprised though that I could do this.

When I told my Area Manager about the horse drawn she was over the moon with this, and a sense of déjà vu came full cycle again.

The difference this time was that my Area Manager made sure I received all the credit as the local Journal headlined - horse drawn funeral procession comes to town. To my surprise, this was the first of its kind in the town for many years, similar to what I had achieved in my previous employment. As had happened before, horse drawn carriages are now common place here as well as they are pretty much all over the Country now.

My stay here was short lived as personal circumstances forced me to return back to Gloucester. To my Area Manager, I have nothing but thanks and praise to her as she believed in me and gave me full backing in whatever I did. I still remain friends with her today.

31. Independent

On my return, I decided to try an independent firm not too far away from where I used to work. It was common knowledge that my new employers didn't care too much for the competition and as I was unfortunately an ex employee of them always knew this was never going to be a match made in heaven.

I knew from the outset I was always going to have a hard time here as the boss was always very critical of everything the competition did, and so I knew that no matter what was asked of me, he would always find an alternative.

As I have got older I have become more patient and tolerant to those that constantly whinge and gripe; some say for an easier life. Well as true as that may be, I really don't enjoy being around people that have absolutely no reason to be negative. I think it important to emphasise at this point that I don't refer to bereaved families in this statement, just people that only have a glass that's half empty outlook on life. For whatever reason the boss was one of these that seemed to spend a lifetime making everyone else miserable. I had spent a few years here but never felt part of the team and so when a position arose with another small business in May 2000 I jumped at the chance.

When I joined Beechwood I didn't know anything about the business as it was a relatively new company set up in 1993. The company had two branches one in Cheltenham and the other in Quedgeley, Gloucester. It was run by the owner and his wife that employed bearers as and when needed which worked well for them. I must admit as I had no insight to their track record I had serious reservations whether this was such a good move, but as I was going absolutely nowhere with my present employment, it was a case of I'll never know unless I try it.

On my interview, the owners had asked me what I wanted from the business. I had got to the age where I had started to get a bit more confident and forthright with my opinions and said that one day I had intended to have my own business. Realising what I had just said, I assumed that the interview was terminated there and then, but it didn't and I sensed that the owners were genuinely interested in my aspirations to which their reply was that they were looking for someone that might one day take over their business.

I don't really know what I was expecting when I said what I did, but it just goes to show, if you don't ask, you don't get (not that I would recommend that line every time). They had family, but none of them were interested in taking the business further as they all had their own careers.

After much talk the owners were sold on my enthusiasm and offered me the job. I started wondering if this was the break I had been waiting for all my working life. Initially I had only gone to agree T & C's and ended up talking about long term plans for taking over the business before I had even officially accepted the offer of employment; I think they call that running before you can walk.

I said I would get back to them by the end of the week as I wanted to check out a few details. When I told a few family members about the offer, naturally there was a lot of scepticism of *sounds too good to be true* or *what do you even know about the company?* Of course these comments and more were fair points to consider as I had thought the same, but I was game for a challenge, and even if nothing came of it, I would still have a job, which was really the whole point in the first place.

I remember the first day like it was yesterday. I couldn't believe how little there was to do, and I was on edge at the fact I was being paid for not doing anything. By the end of the first week I was seriously wondering what on earth I had done and thought that this place surely couldn't be making any money as there was only the one funeral for the week. The boss didn't have a problem with this though and said that they only averaged around two services a week anyway. I began wondering whether the last place was as bad as I had thought – actually, yes it was; and so I had to make the best of what I had here.

It was clear from the off that the boss was okay for me to direct with immediate effect. I fell into the running of Beechwood very quickly and to be fair without trying to teach someone to suck eggs I had been in the profession a lot longer than they had. I was able to direct funerals the way I wanted, unlike the last place where the boss was always hovering over you like a bad smell.

My arrival meant that the owners could leave me in charge running the two offices while they took advantage of a well earned break away. As small and sometimes uneventful as this little business was, there was also something quite right and personal about it, nothing like

I had expected or experienced before. It was a whole new way of funeral directing, and a way I enjoyed. The business made an impression on me and I felt more at home in the first couple of months than I had for the three years previously.

32. Ashes to ashes

When the need arises I can usually think quite quickly on my feet, and never find myself stuck for words – well, for the most part anyway. We had conducted a funeral of an elderly gent a couple of months previous and it was decided his ashes were to be interred in a churchyard in one of the Cotswold villages. This has always been an odd one for me and one that's quite surreal as you are conducting another service albeit less formal for the same person again.

I had the privilege of knowing Bert before he died and he truly was a very nice man. I had popped around his house for a cup of tea and a chat on a couple of occasions and he would tell me of his younger days and the antics he would get up to. He had lied about his age when he joined the Navy as so many had in his day and was always keen to tell me or anyone that would listen about his far flung escapades. He had seen himself as a bit of a ladies' man and was never shy about sharing how many conquests he had had around the world.

I could see Bert was still very much the young man at heart as he would love to reminisce about the glory days. The reality as time take its toll though was now that of a lonely old man holding on to his youth, unaccepting of his advancing years as if it was a cancerous disease.

Every time I had popped around to see Bert, he would always be sat in his armchair that was so old and tatty that the material had worn through to the foam base beneath, watching his favourite program - the channel 4 racing and puffing away on his cigar shaped roll up. The ashtray was resident on the arm of the chair, but rarely would any ash get that far as it usually fell off onto his lap burning another black hole in his trousers.

I couldn't always stay too long but was always welcomed with a cuppa, rich tea biscuit and the offer of a smoke. Naturally I always declined the 'smoke' as I had a job to breathe in the confined space anyway. I think the sell by date on the biscuits were well past their best as well as they were quite often soft to the bite, but I still showed my gratitude and respectfully ate it anyway even if it did remind me of a soggy Farley's Rusk.

I have no idea how he managed to live and breathe in there as you could quite literally cut the air with a knife. Bert was probably on 60 a day and unless you were sat within ten feet of him you probably wouldn't have seen him at all.

Inevitably, whatever our mode of demise is, we all end up the same way and it was of no surprise when I received the sad news of Bert's passing due to a smoke related disease. For all the best advice in the world and what we should and shouldn't do for a healthier life style, at the end of the day, does it really matter? Bert died at the age of 87 and had smoked ever since he was 15. I am not suggesting it is right to go against the advice of those that know better, but in this day and age it seems that no matter what we do, there will always be someone telling us one thing or another. If Bert had never smoked in his life, he may have lived longer or he may not; no one will ever know. It's all about choices we make, and Bert had lived a full life and lived it his way, and as far as I am concerned, what more could anyone ask?

I had prepared a little plot in the churchyard where Bert's ashes were to be interred and waited a short while for the small gathering of family to arrive along with the vicar of the church.

As we stood around the plot the vicar asked me to pour Bert's ashes into the hole which I did mindful of standing upwind of any draft.

The vicar continued in his committal prayer, *'earth to earth, ashes to ashes, dust to dust: in sure and certain hope of the resurrection to eternal life through our Lord Jesus Christ......*

As he closed the committal prayer with *'Amen'* he asked if anyone wanted to say anything as we all stared mesmerizingly at Bert's ashes below. The Grandson Robin not being able to resist the moment commented how surprised he was to see so many ashes and finished *'Our Granddad really loved his fags'*. The moment was an absolute classic as the vicar was left so uncomfortably at a loss for words you could feel him squirming in his cassock trying to think what he should say in response to that. He didn't need to as the rest of the family laughed a moment later once the penny had dropped of what Robin had just said. I am pretty certain Bert would have seen the funny side as well.

33. Dad moves to Hungary

I had been at Beechwood for a couple of years when Dad announced that he wanted to return to his homeland to be with his ageing siblings before it was too late. I must admit, even though he had said on many occasions before, that he would go back home one day, I had assumed the western way of life for the last 46 years was enough to keep him here to what he had become accustomed to. I guess I was wrong, and I understood his reasoning for his decision.

For him, it wasn't just about being reunited with his family; it was I guess a pilgrimage of soul searching and to bury a few ghosts along the way. For very different reasons, in writing this book, I hope I have been able to do the same.

Dad was 15 years old when he escaped from Hungary during the 1956 uprising that started on 23rd October. He was captured and rounded up in Zalaegerszeg, one of the larger towns in Hungary to be returned via train back home again – of course he never did get on the train and years later had discovered that all those that did were never seen again. I am told that as Dad was queuing with the hundreds of other Hungarians to board the carriages, an old gentleman standing by looked down at Dad and simply said very softly *'run'*.

Dad didn't need to ask why; he just knew that their fate wasn't going to be a good one. The old man was too frail to make any attempt to escape and resigned himself to his inevitable demise. Dad saw an opening in the crowds and made his sharp exit through the alleyways and into the countryside. He had I believe narrowly avoided certain death. On that day, I am sure that the old man must have been his very own guardian angel.

The Russian troops were well positioned on all fronts and executed any Hungarians trying to flee across the border into Austria. Dad had walked the treacherous 40 kilometres from Zalaegerszeg to the border, with many of his countrymen losing their lives along the way. An open field that led the way to freedom into Austria was littered with bodies that lay dead where they were shot by Russian soldiers as they mercilessly gunned down anything that caught their eye from the sentry boxes hidden in the treetops.

Dad had spent three days moving a little at a time crawling over the corpses until he had reached the safety of the small Austrian village of Hagensdorf.

One of the sentry boxes that was responsible for so many atrocities still remains there for all to see today as a stark reminder that this must never happen again.

I had come about this story of events only a couple of years ago and via a second party as Dad never did talk about what had happened all those years ago. If he had said when I was growing up, I am not saying I would have liked him anymore, but at least I would have known why. Now that I am older with my own family, and have a small understanding of what happened in the 1956 revolution, I have at least been able to forgive and make the necessary psychological allowances to continue. My unhappy memories of a child growing up will always be there, but at long last I have been able to confront my demons head on and accept things for what they were.

Dad was a very troubled young man that was physically and mentally abused by his own Father – that much I understand, and for this reason I have been able to close my own doors and move on. For what it's worth, Dad in my mind is a remarkable man, and did the best he could with what he was able to cope with. As the years went by I had seen Dad as more of a friend and I grew to like and respect him a lot. When he left England for the last time, I wished him well.

He returned home the 'prodigal son'. To most that knew him, he was a hero – I just wished he had been mine.

34. A new start

2003 was the start of a new beginning for me. After three short years of working for the company, I was offered the chance to buy the owners out. I know I had always wanted to do this for real one day, but I guess that was in the safety of my own mind knowing opportunities like that don't come around every day to people like me with my background.

I was successful in convincing a bank that I was good for the money and they released the monies I needed to buy the company outright. I was still short of the monies I would need for the initial cash flow and so I approached my mortgage lender for a £10,000.00 loan for home improvements. Looking back, I was grateful for the oversight in their loans department for not realising they had already given me a home improvements loan the year before.

Now I had the chance to enter the big time and swim with all the other fish in the sea. The one unnerving fact that was overwhelming was that I would now be the one making business decisions and suddenly felt as if I shouldn't be there. After all, all of the other businesses had a long pedigree of one generation handing over to another, and here I was the first in my family starting from scratch even if I was time served and well respected by my fellow professionals.

I had received many well intentioned messages of support when I took over in the August of 2003 from suppliers and what would now be my competitors. The biggest stumbling block came no soon as I had taken over. The agent for the landlady in the Cheltenham branch had given me a three month notice to vacate the premises. This was my own fault as I was so naive not to have clarified the position of the tenancy before I took over.

The first week was so manic that I just couldn't get my head around all that I had done and became so overwhelmed I almost gave up before I got going. This was by far the most enormous wrench from normality I had ever experienced in my life as I was immediately thrust into a very unenviable and uncertain future. At this stage in my life, this was as lonely a place as I would hope never to find myself again. As far as feeling scared and vulnerable, it surpassed everything I had ever known – I had lost close family members; I had gone through a divorce and I had known the hardships of money worries, yet none of this came anywhere near to the desperate anxiety I now found myself in, because I really was on my own with no one to turn to should I need someone to help bail me out if things went wrong, and it cast me into a depth of fear that I was about to lose everything I had worked so hard to get in the first place.

The ten thousand pounds I had borrowed went in the first week and I had only pennies left to my name – 12 to be exact. I could hardly ask for an overdraft seven days into trading and the desperate feeling of getting it all so wrong made me feel quite physically sick to the pit of my stomach.

So here I was on the verge of bankruptcy before I even started. I had taken on a huge business loan, remortgaged my home again for a cash flow and now facing the inevitable loss of the main branch in Cheltenham to trade from.

Even though I had arranged and conducted a couple of funerals in my first week, it is quite normal that you have to wait for around a month, sometimes much longer for the money to come back in, as it is usually tied up with the deceased estate. Solicitors with all the best will in the world are never that forthcoming in releasing the funds. Insurances are equally as drawn out and even when families are not dealing with either, it is normal practice as per T & C's to give the statutory 21 days to receive payment in full. The one problem you never want to face is someone not paying at all, which for the time being I was at least spared this stumbling block.

I was needless to say relieved to be paid for the first funeral after just a week which gave me a much welcomed temporary reprieve. It gave me the monies I needed to pay for disbursements and services on funerals I had arranged for the coming week, like vicars and doctors fees, florists, crematorium fees and suppliers like the coffin manufacturers.

When you are new to business, it is very difficult to start negotiating with suppliers monthly accounts with no credit rating. I had known Bette from the coffin manufacturers and Brian from the florists since joining Beechwood and they were as good as gold with me, both ordering me not to worry too much about paying their invoices for the time being. Bette and Brian both said at different times that I could have 3 months credit if I needed. Their words of support were gratefully received as I knew both were being so very genuine. Once upon a time they too had jumped into the uncertain world of self employment owning and running a business and knew how difficult it was going to be for me.

I have always paid my way, and even though I could have taken advantage of their kind offers, I still cleared any invoices as soon as I could. If you don't, the debt doesn't go away and I am not one for owing money to anyone. The most important thing you realise very quickly when you are on your own is that you find out who your friends really are; Bette and Brian were and still are very good friends of mine and I am eternally grateful to both.

I don't think I slept once through the night in the early years constantly finding myself pacing the living room floor in the early hours of the morning wondering how on earth I was going to get through the next financial day. Some days I was that thin on cash flow I could only put in enough fuel to cover the day.

Concerned with my anxieties I had offloaded my worries to Bette one day just for someone to talk to. She had said that it was quite normal what I was going through, and that she still paced the sitting room floor herself in the early hours, years on from when they first started. This gave me some relief knowing I wasn't the only one to have gone through this and it did give me some temporary respite, regrettably though there is no escape and it goes part and parcel with the territory.

One major issue I had to address urgently was that while still trying desperately to hang on to my sanity learning how to run a business and working every possible hour in the day to make ends meet, I also had to find another premises to trade from in town.

Whatever people's beliefs are, I believe that there is always someone looking out for you, and as good fortune would have it a property did come to my attention as I drove around the outskirts of town. It was a shop in a parade almost tailor made for my needs in a nice respectable residential area. The shop had been empty for some time and so it was available with immediate effect once all the lease agreements were agreed. It was another expense I could ill afford with a costly solicitors bill, but one that was also unavoidable.

I have no idea how I coped back then as I must have just gone into autopilot, completely tunnel visioned with the determination I wasn't going to be beaten. Moving house is bad enough, but I had to move a business lock, stock and barrel from one side of town to another and run it as well. With the much needed help of family we were able to transfer everything from the one site to the other over the next few weeks, leaving the refrigeration cabinet until the last.

Just like moving home you have to notify so many people like banks, utilities, telephone, insurances, councils, etc etc. Moving a business is this and ten times more as you now have to establish a new base. You have to change all your paperwork, long term advertising; tell all of your suppliers, write to inform all of your clients of a change of address – the list is endless, and believe me it is a task not to be taken lightly unless you have the infrastructure to cope with it, which I didn't, as I pretty much ran on a shoestring budget in those early days.

Eventually after so much effort, the new branch was fully operational, and to be fair a much better place than the previous one. I had one problem though – the residents committee took a dislike to a funeral parlour opening up in the parade and petitioned the council to have me removed. I had already been granted permission to trade there by the council as I had met all the criteria and passed with flying colours. This didn't stop the objections though and when the committee realised I was all above board and legal, decided to take things into their own hands by making abusive telephone calls saying that I wasn't welcome here and that I should go elsewhere.

I received quite a number of calls like this to start with and I can't deny it, it really did upset me as I seemed to deal with one major problem after another - goodness knows how I didn't fold from mental exhaustion back then. If it wasn't from the objectors, some mornings I would arrive at work to find graffiti over the windows or chips and curry sauce smeared into the window frontage, sometimes worse!

You know, looking back now, I do wonder why I even bothered in the first place. Eventually the objectors backed off and the graffiti stopped too. One of the other shop owners had confided in me, that it was nothing personal; the residents committee objected to any new business that came here – it was what they did. The graffiti was a separate issue altogether as a group of youths from another estate were well known for targeting new shops in the area really just to appease their own boredom, even if it was at my expense.

I think one of the most disheartening things for me, was that here I was trying to provide a service for people that one day everyone will use and at the same time being disrespected from every angle either in the form of verbal abuse or damage caused by youths with their marker pens and aerosols.

If that wasn't enough having to contend with the upheavals of my Cheltenham base, the Gloucester base was ordered by the landlord for a complete damp proof course which basically shut down the shop for 5 long weeks. I was only 3 months into running a business and I think whatever could of gone wrong certainly did. The only saving grace was that I didn't have to pay any rent for the time the Gloucester office was out of action. I will never know how much work I had potentially lost for that time, but was mighty glad when it was up and running again.

Back in Cheltenham a new shop in the parade opened a couple of doors away, which prompted a new interest to the objectors. I had now become old news, and I for one was quite happy about that. One of the main objectors even started to walk past my shop window again who had previously made the point of crossing the road just to let me know she wasn't happy with my presence here. On the first funeral that was arranged from the estate I operated in, quite a good number from the locality attended the service including some of my biggest fan base (the residents committee) and for the first time they could see what I was all about and how I operated my business.

I bleed the same as anyone else, I laugh and cry just like everyone else and apart from the job I do, nor am I any different to anyone else. This was the first time they could see face to face what I was all about.

The word had got around after that and the grapevine certainly served its purpose as I was now being slowly accepted as part of the community even if it did take the best part of nine months to convince them.

It had taken almost a year before the Cheltenham branch started to establish itself and as hard as it was, proved to be a blessing in disguise even if it didn't seem like it at the time.

35. Accents

I think it fair to say, I am quite typical of the West Country and have a fairly distinguishable accent to match. You know it really is impossible to talk posh with a Gloucester accent so there is no point in trying.

I have no problem with the class structure in this Country and I know that I can get along fine with anyone just so long as they can put up with me. I treat everyone the same which is why I think I am well suited for the job I do. The one thing I can quite proudly say is that I never try to be anything more or less than I am. If I say I will do something I will, and look after all of the families I serve equally. As someone once said of me referring to a well known brand of exterior preservative, *'you're like that varnish on telly'* - slightly baffled I said *'I'm sorry I don't follow'*. *'You do exactly what it says on the tin'* came the reply. Not the most complimentary statement in the world I grant you but I knew what he meant and it was gratefully received.

It is generally accepted that the funerals you arrange are from the surrounding locality (not that there is a given 'patch' that we all have to stick to) and from time to time can quite unexpectedly get a call from a family nowhere near the area you normally work in.

One afternoon out of the blue I received a call from a family in the Cotswolds about 20 miles away that asked if I could help them with the funeral arrangements for their Father who had died. The family were from Down Under but staying with friends while here at a beautiful manor in the country set in its own private grounds.

I was greeted by one of the sons who despite his sad loss was very warm and welcoming. I felt immediately at ease with him and the entire family as we gathered in one of the reception rooms to go through the details.

I would be the first to admit that when it comes to current affairs, I am not exactly going to score many points on who's who. This has always been to my advantage though as I have never had any preconceived ideas of anyone and treat everyone the same.

As we were chatting, there was a very positive mood in the room which seems typical of everyone I have ever met from the southern hemisphere. Drinks were on offer of the alcoholic type, maybe I guess to ease any tensions they had, but never did anything get out of hand, just a very relaxed somewhat weird arrangement as I was beginning to wonder if I was being disrespectful by being too 'British'.

I wasn't overly comfortable with the relaxed mood of everyone and hoped I didn't offend anyone by not allowing myself to enter into the same manner as they. This wasn't the first time I had dealt with families from that part of the world and they did all seem to be quite consistent in their positive outlook on life.

After a while their attention turned on me as I was very audibly different to the people they would normally mix with. One of the family joked as he said to me in a very cross plummy Oz accent *'I say you don't exactly speak with the Queens English'*. As sharp as a pin I answered in my usual Gloucester accent *'no I'm afraid I'm one of the peasants, I can't be doing with all that marbles in the mouth talk'*.

It was as if a whole weight was lifted at my reply and I was now the affection of everyone's amusement, (strange people I thought – hadn't they heard a commoner before?) Even the lady that had looked on unjudgingly from the side of the room all the while I was there smiled kindly as if to acknowledge acceptance. I am not normally slow to pick up on things, but I just didn't get the joke and so cautiously carried on being careful not to give rise to any other comments that would get a laugh.

I left none the wiser over what I had said and when I got back to base started to make phone calls to get things moving. The widow had decided she wanted her husband at the manor for the few days before the funeral took place and so I arranged for a couple of bearers to help me take her husband back.

When we pulled up outside the manor we were again greeted by her sons who even helped us to carry their Dad into the reception room where he was to stay on view for those that wanted to pay their last respects to him. Once I was happy that everything was all okay, I reiterated to the family that if they had any concerns whatsoever, night or day, they must call me. I am always on tender hooks when families want their loved ones at home as you are always thinking the worst. What if the coffin falls off the trestles, What if there is a sudden change in appearance that upsets the family, what if.......? You could be wondering all night long, and usually did, but it doesn't make the day come any quicker, it just makes the night even longer.

The family assured me that they had everything in hand, and thanked me for all my help. I left slightly more at ease than when I went in as they certainly seemed to be okay with all the arrangements.

As we drove down the gravelled drive my one bearer said to me as if I should know *'Do you have any idea who those people are?' 'Not a clue?'* I replied wondering how he could have known anymore than me considering I had made all of the arrangements. Not being able to contain his knowledge any longer said again *'you really don't know who they are do you?' 'Nope you've got me there; I really don't know who they are'.*

He went on to say that the family whose manor it was, were one of the richest families in the Country.

'Well' I said *'that's very impressive'. 'I don't think you know how rich they are?'* he said as if I should be in awe of his statement. *'They own half of Regent Street'. 'Wow'* I said as I started to count how many houses there were in Regent Street, Gloucester. *'Not Regent Street, Gloucester'* he laughed, *'Regent Street, London – what's more they are well known amongst the Royals'*

At this jaw dropping moment, I cast my memory back to the comment I had made about the Queens English and the amusement it brought to the whole family in the arrangement.

'Well, there goes my MBE' I said wondering if there would be any repercussions of my inappropriate comments.

It turned out the lady that had said nothing all the while I was there was in fact a real Lady; one Lady Eleanor Barrington. I remembered her only as someone who had taken a back seat in the arrangements with no input other than I guess moral support - how wrong I was. Prior to the funeral Lady Eleanor called me a couple of times just to make sure everything was still as planned. I assured her it was and said that I would next see her when we were to attend the proceedings of the funeral.

When we arrived on the day of the funeral which was held in the open grounds of the estate, the first person to greet me was Lady Eleanor. Before the service was to begin she did take me to one side and thanked me for being just 'normal' and not trying to be someone I wasn't. It was a really nice compliment and I thanked her for her sincerity. I think I was probably a breath of fresh air, and even I could now see the funny side of what I had said about the Queens English. However I am still in no doubt that I might be waiting a very long time before I get a tap on the shoulder.

Lady Eleanor enforced everything I already knew about high society and the super rich – that they are just genuinely really nice people born of a life style that wasn't of their choosing. Goodness knows I wouldn't want their life, but then I guess they equally probably wouldn't want mine.

Despite the circumstances, all in all it was an extremely pleasurable experience, and there was a mutual appreciation from both tiers of class.

36. The Big Taboo

It was only thirty years ago, but 'Death' was a big taboo even then. For some reason it was considered bad luck to talk about it. People don't feel comfortable talking about things they don't understand. Religion is a perfect example. Most have no understanding of it at all and therefore Vicar and Church could be as alien as teaching someone a foreign language for the first time. You might be able to read chapter and verse from the Bible but have no idea what you just said.

People's perceptions of what we must be have usually given the outsider the misguided imagery largely thanks to black and white horror movies of the Boris Karloff era, that we should resemble the same stereotyped gaunt looks, deep set eyes, bony features and pale off white skin tones. Why then would anyone want to come within ten feet of an Undertaker? After all they must surely not be normal.

Welcome to my world!

I can assure everyone that there is no real mystery, none that I am aware of anyway. We are born into this world, we live in this world and when our body or mind has worn out we leave this world. The only mystery there is, is that none of us know the when and where – Thank goodness!

In recent years I have done many talks to groups like WI, the over 60's clubs, Probus etc. etc breaking down the myths of death. In short, I say to people if you want to know something, and I can answer it, I will tell you. In truth the reality is nowhere as graphic as people imagine. For the most part it can sometimes be quite uneventful with not too much going on. The whole purpose of the talks was to give people an awareness and understanding of who we are and what we do. In general, I am sure we in the funeral profession are probably more sensitive to real life than any other profession you could name and yet be as popular as a taxman for the Inland Revenue – however, to date I am not aware of any taxmen giving up their time to give a talk to an elderly group in a village hall for free – but there again why would they?

Talks have always gone down well with the groups I have been to and I have always been lucky enough that at least one or two always enjoyed being the mouthpiece for the group which would give me a rhetoric springboard to bounce off in an open forum. I always encouraged this style of talk as it would usually result in people being far more educated and informed than before. Those that usually came to my talks had a general interest in what I do, but were always too afraid to ask the question for fear of embarrassment. The talks were aimed at making us more accessible to the public in exactly the same way that today's Doctors and Vicars are also.

When people take a moment to see that I eat and breathe, laugh and cry at the same things everyone else does; listen to Radio 2, watch soaps on TV (okay, maybe I went too far there), drink tea with milk and not embalming fluid, then the mystical veil that had once enveloped much of the funeral directors persona becomes exposed and our profile made accessible to people who see that we are not so different after all. Contrary to what anyone might think my last name isn't Time and nor do I own a scythe or wear a full length hoodie – not even on cold nights! I have never received any negative feedback from such talks and was always delighted when some groups asked me to go back the next year for those that chose not to be there for the fear I might have had an ulterior motive in looking for premature customers.

After doing a few talks around the County, you get a feel for the type of questions people will throw at you in the open forum. We as people are uniquely different in every way and the decisions we make in everyday life makes us who and what we are. Yet as individual as we would all like to think we are, some of the things we say and do are as predictable as day and night. The questions tended to be the same from one talk to another which endorsed the fact that regardless of intellect or age, we generally all think the same way. What we don't know or understand, we make up and pass down the line to the next generation of thought. We ask questions in a way that we think no one has ever asked before assuming there to be no answer. After a while I could usually predict the cross flow of questioning and usually knew what was coming next before it was even asked, but always made sure I didn't get too eager in cutting someone off in their prime as it was for their entertainment as much as mine. Sometimes the talks went so well that if the audience hadn't known everyone there, it would have been conceivable to think I had brought along my own heckler. That's the fun part knowing the answer before they finish.

Typical questions would be what happens to the gold rings in cremation? Quite simply nothing, as all soft metals are left untraceable through the cremation process. The only compounds to withstand such temperatures from the cremation are the titanium hip and knee implants, which are disposed of after cremation by the crematorium staff in an undisclosed area that not even Funeral Directors know the whereabouts of. Families do of course reserve the right to retain these parts – I have never come across such a request yet, but I guess there is always a first!

Are coffins sold back to the funeral directors for re-using?

This one always makes me smile as I cannot honestly believe people actually think this. Do people really imagine delivery vans turning up at the crematorium every day to recycle the coffins back to the funeral directors? No doubt at some point I will be asked if coffins can be bought on eBay; maybe I shouldn't speak to soon.

Can more than one body be cremated at a time?

Again another misplaced myth and the answer is no, each cremation is carried out separately. However, exceptions can be made in the case of a mother and baby or small twin children, so long as the next of kin or executor has made this specific request. A cremator can only accept one coffin at a time and all the remains are removed from the cremator before the next cremation takes place, and yes the coffin is cremated with the body. An identity card is used throughout the whole process until the final disposal, thereby ensuring correct identification.

What is the percentage between cremation and burial in the UK?

Since 1968 when the number of cremations exceeded burials for the first time, cremation has increased considerably. Current figures suggest that around 70% of all funerals are cremations.

What is the temperature of a cremation?

Before a coffin can be cremated the cremator needs to be brought up to operating temperature. This temperature is in the region of 850-900 °C for the primary chamber. The secondary chamber must be above 850 Celsius at all times during the cremation to keep within the environmental law requirements. This law is in place due to the gases which are produced from the cremation. The gases generated such as carbon monoxide can be burnt off at or above this minimum temperature and therefore reduce the emissions which are passed into the atmosphere

Is it true that hair continues to grow after someone dies?

No. The appearance of growth, is due to dehydration, muscle atrophy (partial or complete wasting away of a muscle), and retraction of the top layers of skin.

I have never felt any need to go into any more depth than this as people have usually come just to be entertained and not frightened the life out of. My talks have never been about the technical or unpleasant side that naturally goes with the territory, but put into simple terms that people might understand, and generally those that have asked questions, walk away all the more enlightened than before.

37. Awareness

A good friend of mine Steve Hooper nicknamed 'Trooper' (I assume from his chain smoking) is also a Funeral Director and had gone through the same baptism of fire as myself with owning and running a business. One day he told me of a funeral that he had conducted up in London just recently. My one big regret was that I wished I had been there to see it. If there hadn't been so many witnesses including his own bearers I am sure he would never have told the tale – I know I wouldn't!

We all from time to time travel distances to other areas outside our comfort zones to conduct funerals in other parts of the Country. Sat Nav's have taken away some of the guess work you would need to find your destination without concern for where you were going. I for one will be the first to admit I do rely quite heavily on technology as an aid to making the job easier and have no embarrassment sharing this. Who cares if we live in a world where the dashboard computer tells us *'after 300 yards take the next left'*. If at the end of the journey it says *'you have reached your destination'* and you look up to see you have, then I am more than happy to embrace the 21st century and all it has to offer.

Steve and his staff had to go to North London some 100 miles away to conduct a funeral he had arranged the week before. All set and armed only with a Sat Nav and a packet of sandwiches, Steve and his men set off without any concerns or worries for the journey ahead. Amusingly along their route the Sat Nav also picked up and alerted the hearse driver of approaching speed cameras – not that they were travelling that fast anyway.

As Steve and his bearers pulled up outside the church in good time, mourners were already filing in giving their names to a funeral reporter as they entered. Steve introduced himself to the daughter who had arranged the funeral the week before and she in turn introduced him to the rest of the family. As people were still gathering, Steve told the principal mourners that he would just pop into the church to familiarise himself with the layout and to make himself known to the vicar and make sure everything, including trestles were in place.

The church was now nearly full with around two hundred plus people already seated. There were just a few minutes left before the service was to start when Steve caught sight of the vicar and walked over to meet him and give him his fees.

It's of great comfort to know that when you are out of your area and everything runs like clockwork, you are graciously reminded of how important it was to thoroughly examine every aspect of the arrangement before you left. Quite deservedly you give yourself a little pat on the back at your attention to detail as to all and sundry for those present who wouldn't know you hadn't been there a hundred times before. The principal mourners outside the church were now all ready to proceed and with everyone in place the vicar led the coffin into the church just as the bells chimed in the hour. It's great when that happens; it makes all of the preparation worth the while whether it was intentional or just kind coincidence.

Proudly, Steve led the bearers and family down the side aisle toward the chancel step where the pall bearers would rest the coffin. This was one of those churches where you would walk across the front pews to the alter so that the congregation were immediately to your right as oppose to entering the church from the back. The bearers placed the coffin on the trestles, bowed to the alter and awaited Steve to give them the nod to leave.

As the bearers left; the church warden closed the door behind them to keep the heat in. Steve stayed just a few more moments just to make sure he was happy everything was okay before turning to also leave the church.

This was the moment that I would have paid a large amount of money to see what happened next. Steve left the church in full view of the two hundred strong congregation through what he thought was the outside door.

The door he left through was in fact no more than the broom cupboard and storeroom. As Steve walked into the cupboard he realised his mistake with immediate horror but spared his embarrassment by staying put not wanting to be the centre of attraction; he had also noticed that the vicar had momentarily paused his words of scripture in mid flight as if he had forgotten his lines – but he hadn't and there was now an uncomfortable silence as if the church was empty – except it wasn't.

Those couple of seconds of silence must have seemed like a lifetime to Steve as he listened intently at the door and now realising what everyone in church must now be thinking. Unable to make good of a bad situation he decided to grind out the entire service sat on Harry the Hoover.

Steve waited for the last hymn to get into full verse before making his entrance again. Those that were closest to the door chuckled as he walked by; even the vicar couldn't resist a nod and a wink.

If Steve hadn't taken his staff on that day, no one would ever have known. I for one am mighty glad he did, as it was such a great story.

Pause for thought: In this day and age we use technology to get us anywhere in the world right to the very doorstep. Finding your way back out might just require a little observation.

38. A question of taste

Not so very many years ago it was always a done thing, almost as if a legal doctrine that everyone had a dignified religious service usually in Church first with one or two hymns and then on to either the graveside or crematorium for a final prayer of committal and blessing. The very suggestion of popular music at a funeral then was considered totally disrespectful and inappropriate. Of course nowadays it has almost reversed; most funeral services today are held at the local crematorium as more and more people are turning away from what was traditional. Crematorium services have simplified the process of saying our 'Goodbyes' by holding everything in one place (some say too simple) but it is a fact that people's ideas about how we say farewell to a loved one now concentrates more about the person and how they would have liked to have been remembered than a religious organisation dictating what they believed to be appropriate.

It is quite the norm that a piece of music as chosen by the family will be played on entry and exit from the chapel. Over the years people have become more and more adventurous with what is considered acceptable. I think I have heard every type of music genre requested at services and it would be fair to say there appears to be no limits as to what lengths some families will go to. If after careful consideration they are still happy with their choice in music then that is all that matters, although I would go as far to say there are some vicars that do have quite a strong opinion about this.

If you can believe it, there is even a current top ten list of popular songs played at funerals.

Of all the decisions that need to be made in arranging a funeral, the two areas that always seem to cause a mental block with the nearest and dearest are what flowers to have and the choice of song that will be relevant to the person that had died but not so outlandish as to offend any senior members of the congregation.

If I am allowed one bit of advice for the generation to come is that rather than leave it to second guess what music you would wish is to write it down and tell someone. I consider myself fairly in touch with the modern popular music scene but don't really think that much of it would be appropriate for what is me. Over the years I have picked out four tracks for myself that I would like played which I still listen to regularly today and unless I completely overkill the CD's on my car stereo ones that I would still want when the time comes. They are, but not in any specific order: Neil Diamond singing Hava Nagila (live version), Hungarian Dance No5 by Brahms, Sunrise, Sunset from the soundtrack 'Fiddler on the roof' and Sibelius' Finlandia.

Some of the most popular and requested pieces of music that pop up on a regular basis are Andrea Bocelli and Sarah

Brightman singing Time To Say Goodbye, Eric Clapton and Tears In Heaven, Angels by Robbie Williams, Frank Sinatra and My Way, The Righteous Brothers singing Unchained Melody, Tina Turner belting out Simply The Best, My Heart Will Go On by Celine Dion, Elton John with Candle In The Wind and so on.

Controversially some people have steered a little left of centre and raised an eyebrow or two with ones like:

The Jam singing Going Underground, Dr and the Medics with Spirit In The Sky, the classic Led Zeppelin singing Stairway To Heaven (I have always made sure this is played at the end of the service as it is such a long song), same goes for Bat Out Of Hell by Meatloaf. Blue Oyster Cult singing (Don't Fear) The Reaper is yet another great tune. Humorous tracks like Monty Pythons Always Look On The Bright Side Of Life. I did worry over this track the first time It was requested and asked the vicar if he was okay with it particularly as one of the lines in the song wasn't really appropriate and I thought it might embarrass him. He replied with a big smile *'nonsense, the life of Brian is one of my favourite films of all time'*. A more contemporary song by Green Day singing Good Riddance (Time Of My Life) is actually a very good song which I like a lot.

There were two occasions both of which I took the service in favour of the family wanting a vicar when even I felt so uncomfortable with the song choice that I felt like swapping places with the person in the coffin. Sometimes I find it hard to understand what people are thinking of. The first occasion was the family that wanted The Doors singing Light My Fire. I did suggest a different track might be more appropriate but the husband insisted that his wife would have wanted that and so we did. The second occasion was by far the worst and I will never forget it as long as I live as I hope never to get asked that again. Even I have to admit that as far as the saying goes *'a time and a place for everything'*, the crazy world of Arthur Brown singing Fire in a crematorium service is definitely not the right time or place for that. People have the right to choose whatever they want but the next time I get that request; I will regrettably have to pass on it.

So the next time you are thinking of what music to have played in the funeral and you think you will shock the funeral director, just remember, we have probably heard it all before. In case you think we haven't here are a few more tracks that I have had suggested to me that haven't been played... yet!

Queen – Another One Bites The Dust

Berlin – Take My Breath Away

Jamiriquoi – Going Deeper Underground

Amii Stewart – Knock On Wood

Foreigner – Cold As Ice

Bee Gees – Staying Alive and last but by no means least

AC/DC and Highway To Hell

39. Changing opinions

When I started out, there was really only one type of funeral and that was religious. Today we have so many alternatives that an arrangement that was once achievable in twenty minutes now takes a couple of hours just to go through everything that is available to your client.

I guess it is really the last five years or so that has seen an explosion in alternative choices. Every avenue as far as I can see has been explored, though I am sure what we have to date will not be the end of what is still to come.

I was very privileged to have been involved in the reintroduction of horse drawn carriages in my earlier days as a Funeral Director and did wonder if I could cap this.

I had now become established in my new premises in Cheltenham when such a request not only emulated the horse drawn theme but far exceeded it with the other personal wishes that were requested.

The funeral was to be of a local musician that played in a jazz band; there was also the request for a bamboo coffin which is basically natural bamboo stripped and intertwined into a basket style weave. The beauty about bamboo is that not only is it the fastest living plant in the world and also the strongest; it is absolutely eco friendly to the environment. The fact that it is imported from China would argue the point that the carbon footprint would actually contradict this statement. Apparently though, because of the way they are shipped (one inside the other like Russian dolls), it equates to each coffin using the equivalent to less than a gallon of petrol, and just one for the naturists out there, it is also only made from a type of bamboo that Panda's don't eat.

This funeral procession was to be my crowning glory to date as not only did it surpass my expectations of what can be achieved, it also caused the town as we paraded through to come to a bit of a standstill, with lots of people taking photos on their mobile phones as we walked through.

As we assembled on the busy ring road in the town centre there was already a lot of interest in what was going on. The four members of the Ideal Jazz Band had versed me on what they did and the pace to which they would walk just so that I wouldn't go too far in front. What the Conductor didn't tell me was that as his four piece band marched and played, he would sometimes pop in a jig along the way and quite at random add a little hop, skip and click of his heels in mid air. I can't deny it I did feel slightly unprepared for that and wondered if I was supposed to follow suit. As much as the temptation was to do the same as the music played behind, anyone that knows me, will know that I have two left feet, and any idea of me trying to attempt what the Conductor was doing would have I am sure ended in me scraping myself off the floor.

Most funeral services from when you leave base to its conclusion last around two hours. By the time we had walked through the centre of town, stopping all proceedings on the way, had the church service and then finally finishing with the burial which took place some twenty miles away in a natural woodland burial site had now clocked up around six hours and we were all naturally exhausted from our work which was accomplished to the highest degree of success. I must point out, that the horse drawn carriage didn't travel the twenty miles from the church to the burial ground. Their duties finished in town and we had transferred the bamboo coffin onto our hearse after the service in church for this part of the journey.

The mourners had hired a 52 seater coach for their trip to the natural burial ground accompanied by the ever jovial jazz band that entertained along the way playing tunes like 'Sweet Georgia Brown' and 'When The Saints Go Marching On' to name but a couple.

A natural burial ground is exactly as you imagine. There are no headstones permissible here, just natural woodland. A tree is planted to commemorate the position of the plot and when the tree becomes established a simple bird box could be placed on one of the branches. The field is usually planted with wild flowers which encourage natural habitat and wildlife hence giving the name Natural Woodland Burials. It's not every ones cup of tea, as some woodland areas are still in their infancy and have not yet matured. A new woodland site can be nothing more than an open field that is overgrown with weeds and not too much in the way of wildlife either. If you can imagine what it might look like in twenty years or so then I think it might make the traditionalist a little more convinced that this is actually not a bad concept, that is if you're into burials – me personally, I am not. In fact I am not too keen on any way, but I had read recently on another mode of funeral that was pioneered and patented by biologist Susanne Wiigh-Mäsak in Sweden in 1997 called 'promession'.

In simple terms it is freeze dried funerals. This involves the body being immersed into a chamber of liquid nitrogen at minus 196 degrees. The body then becomes instantly solid and brittle and with a subtle vibration the body breaks down into a powder form. The powder is then dried reducing the deceased remains to around 30% of their original body weight. All metals are then removed before the final remains are placed in a bio degradable casket for interment.

Not that I am going to want to rush this idea for myself, but I do see this as a more effective way of disposal. The plus side to all this, is that there are no emissions, and that can only be good for the environment. Don't get too excited though about being more efficient – apparently the process will cost around the same as cremation. We have a long way to go before it will be passed through our governing laws, but one that I am sure will inevitably come.

I have already mentioned Bamboo coffins, but there are now so many different types of coffin made from all sorts of materials that the common wood veneer will in the not too far distant future play second fiddle to every other type available.

Some of the alternatives coffins that are already on the market are ones made from banana leaf, water hyacinth (an aquatic plant whose leaves are woven in the same way as with banana leaf), sea grass, cane, coco sticks, loom which is made from long yarns of paper, the more traditional willow also wool, cotton, cardboard, recycled newspapers. New products are coming into the market all the time as there seems to be a never ending challenge to experiment with every type of material. Some of the most colourful coffins to hit the market are exactly that – colourful. Among the 1001 generic designs to choose from there is also a facility to completely design your very own bespoke images on the coffin which are then lithographically lasered on to the coffin exterior. As inappropriate as this might sound, in reality the finished product is nothing less than astounding as I found out for myself at one of the funeral exhibitions in Stoneleigh recently.

Let's not stop here. The traditional hearse that we all know has on occasion been substituted in favour of a motorcycle and side car hearse; there is also a VW Camper and Land Rover Jeep conversion hearse for those wanting a complete change from the norm.

For those not too worried about money, then why not consider letting go of around £ 3,000 and having your loved ones ashes turned into diamonds. (The process here involves converting the carbon of ashes to make a real diamond in a laboratory, but instead of millions of years in the making, takes just a few months).

If you really want to go out on a big bang, then maybe the thought of your ashes being part of a firework display might light your fuse. Again this isn't cheap (around £1,000 +). However the thought of being thrust at G-Force into the night sky on the end of a rocket before exploding into a puff of smoke might just be too much for some to comprehend. Certainly not my idea of a night out!

Thought: I've always wanted to go out with a bang! But I would also like my feet to be placed firmly on the ground.

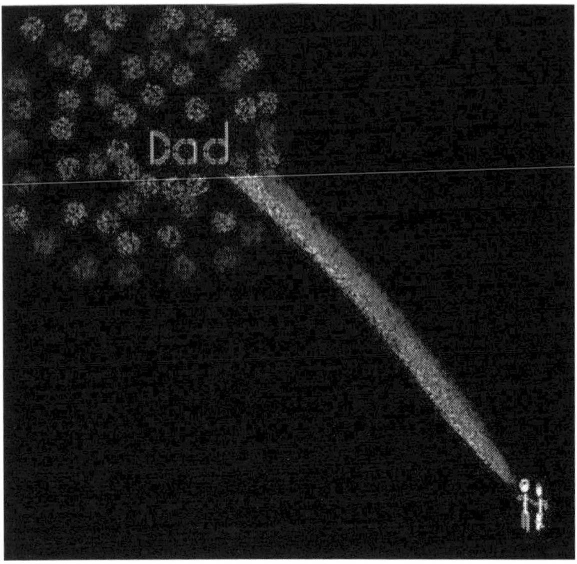
Dad

40. Non Religious

I can remember when the Humanist services started to have a major impact in the County around the mid 1990's. Humanist services are non religious conducted by celebrants. Humanists do not believe in a God or gods, or any other supernatural or divine entities. Humanism is an approach to life based on humanity and reason.

Initially the concept of having a service without a religious minister even to me seemed unnervingly blasphemous and I wasn't sure myself whether it was morally right. Even if the family had no religious belief at all, it just seemed respectful to adhere to this traditional form of doctrine, much the same as the christening of a new born. Our society tells us this is what is socially acceptable and whether we believe or not may not necessarily be the issue, but keeping Granny happy might. For the skeptic, this could be argued to be no more than a conspiracy of mass hypnosis since time began. For the ardent believer it is the only way of salvation to what lies beyond. To those that sit on the fence and don't really care one way or another usually play safe and hedge their bets with a watered down religious service substituting hymns for popular music - just in case there is something, and if there isn't, well it didn't matter anyway.

I wasn't exactly sure what my opinion should be the first time I sat in and listened to a humanist service, half of me expecting the congregation to walk out once they had realised the person taking the service was not wearing a dog collar. There were naturally a few comments from people that weren't too pleased about not having a vicar, but the same could be said about every service I have ever been to – as the saying goes '*you can please some of the people some of the time.....*'.

Originally when the humanist movement exploded onto the funeral scene they seemed quite cautious about their fees and charged much less than the Church of England that was current then, I guess to get a foothold into what has now turned out to be a very lucrative business enterprise. As the humanist movement has grown in popularity so too has their charges and are now substantially much higher than the Anglican fees. It is worth noting at this point that the Catholic Church also fall in line with the Church of England fees. It is really only the more charismatic churches like the Pentecostals, Baptists, and Evangelicals that don't take payment for weddings and funerals. Unfortunately there is a commercial side to everything, but it is at least refreshing to see that the '*happy clappy*' free churches don't charge their members as their infrastructure is more than capable of looking after their own through tithes and offerings.

After sitting through many humanist services in the early years, and pretty much hearing the same thing over and over again, I decided that when the time was right, I would have a go myself. The first time this opportunity came was when I had taken over Beechwood in 2003 and now felt I had enough confidence to stand up and put a little something back into the service.

On the arrangement the family had said that they had heard of these non religious services and asked if I could sort out a humanist to take the service. They had already told me there would only be a handful of people there and so I said, *'well, if you feel comfortable about it, I could do this for you'.*

The family were more than happy with this idea as they had said I knew as much about their Aunt as anyone else would have and so didn't see any point in going over the same material again with someone else, as long as I didn't mind. I assured them I didn't.

I did confirm to them that there would be no fee for me to take the service as I just couldn't justify any charge for providing an additional service to what we were already doing. The family were more than happy with this arrangement and gratefully accepted my offer.

On the day of the funeral, I cannot deny my heart was in my mouth and was now wondering what on earth I had agreed to. All of a sudden I remembered the reason why I had never participated at anything in school when it came to drama or English lessons. It was because I was rubbish at it.

There was no backing out now, and as I nervously approached the lectern and faced the dozen or so mourners, I could feel my heart thumping against the inside of my chest. I had been given a solid piece of advice by a good friend of mine who had told me to speak clearly and take a good breath between sentences and most importantly, take your time.

I did all these things as he had said. I also cued the music in the right place and pressed the right button to close the curtains at the end of the service. When it was over, I felt totally relieved and promised myself I needn't put myself through that kind of pressure again. On a positive note I had confronted my one biggest fear of speaking in public. I was thanked by the family for my part and assured by them that that was exactly what Auntie would have wanted. Needless to say I was ecstatic and on Cloud 9 with the feedback.

Contrary to what I had already told myself, I did take more and more services in favour of employing humanists or celebrants, not because I necessarily wanted to, but because this was something I could do for families without any charge. Over time, word had got around about me taking these types of services and I had now found myself taking them on what was now becoming a regular occurrence. I knew one day the congregations would get bigger, and remember well the first big service that I took when there were in excess of hundred and fifty people. Mentally I had prepared myself for a large congregation but when faced with the reality of what stood before me, all of a sudden the whole event became quite overwhelming. After a few deep breaths as I looked over the wave of mourners filing into the chapel to be seated, I started to regain composure. I had repeatedly reminded myself that apart from the size of the congregation it was no different to all of the smaller funerals I had taken.

To say the experience was nerve racking was a minor understatement particularly when I knew one of the mourners was my bank manager. After the service came to a close and I led the family and congregation out, I was on a different level and had received nothing but appraisal for the type of service it was, and asked by many there if I could give them my number as it was something they too would like one day.

To this day I have not charged so much as a penny and nor do I intend to...not ever. I never advertise the fact that I take services for families that don't require a vicar for the fear that I might be trying to influence someone's decision at a very difficult time. I only offer my services when families request a non religious service. I hope the reason my offer is taken up is not because I don't charge a fee but because that's what they feel comfortable with.

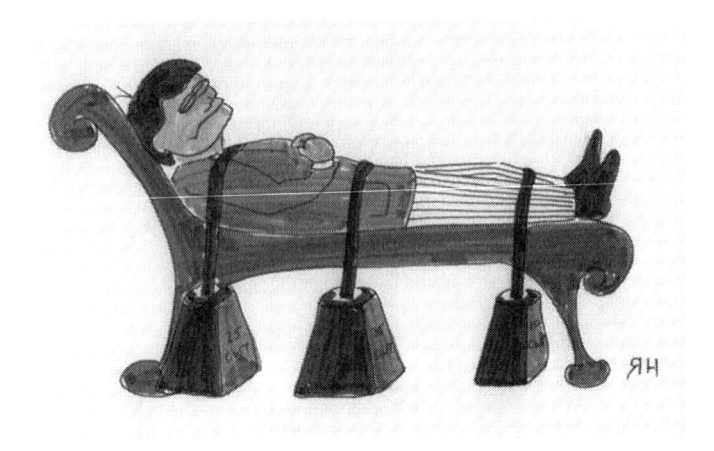

41. Exhaustion

In the April of 2009, I had just come to an end of a relentless three and a half months of solid nonstop work. Now I am not talking about rushed off your feet for eight hours and then doing a bit of overtime on top – I mean twenty hour days, seven days a week for three and a half months. Quite often I would fall asleep at the computer desk and wake up a few hours later to carry on where I had left off.

In plain English, I didn't know my arse from my elbow and for the most part it felt as if someone had whacked me across the side of the head with a sledge hammer. It really is amazing how your body works under stress. Never once did I forget anything in that gruelling time. I was focussed and as sharp as a pin. For what it's worth, I was beginning to think I was indestructible. I kept telling myself that all the aches and pains were psychosomatic and that it was all mind over matter. I had convinced myself that nothing could stop me.

I don't remember that defining point or what event that led to the demise and rapid free fall of my mental state, but do remember that my body and mind had decided enough was enough, and basically stopped. I had no idea of how close I was playing with my own mortality until it was too late.

All of us walk that thin line in everyday life but are blissfully unaware that through one bad decision or course of unfortunate events we are all that close, some closer than others to tipping the balance. I had abused my body and mind for so long and not taken heed of any of the signs that it was inevitable something was going to go wrong. It did go wrong, so very very wrong. In a poorly state of mind I made an appointment to see my doctor who said to come round straight away. The diagnosis was very quick, as he had seen this many times before. I had basically gone into meltdown. He prescribed me tablets that would not be a short term fix, but one that I would be spending a very long time on. He had said that I had basically worn everything out, and that I would need to make some major readjustments in my life to find some sort of normality again. He had also said that I was certainly not to come off the tablets he had given me and was to have regular checkups with him to keep an eye on my progress which on a good day fluctuated between bad and worse.

My doctor was second to none who pointed me in all the right directions and always kept a check on me. He even called me at random times in the day just to see if I was still okay. I assured him I was, but I wasn't really and he knew it. He did refer me to a special unit that deals with the sort of breakdown I had had as I was now out of his comfort zone for what G.P's treat. One contact I had from the clinic was a psychiatrist Dr Annabelle Harper who had really brought me back from the point of despair to a recovery that became more manageable as the months went by with one to one consultations.

When you go through a breakdown, the ones you find the hardest to talk to are your own family as you feel somehow you have failed. Everything I had stood for now seemed worthless. I felt as empty as a hollowed tree trunk – the trunk was the outer body, but the hollow was my soul that felt as if it had been ripped out. I had and still to this day have a very successful business with everything to live for and yet then I would have gladly given it all away just to have my mind back.

My mind had become so exhausted that I just didn't feel like functioning anymore and was quite happy to just disappear. Before this happened, I could never understand how anyone could just lose their mind and walk away from their responsibilities. I used to wonder why anyone could be so damn selfish and would find it hard to show any sympathy towards people that had gone off the rails when they had so much to live for.

As far as sane, dependable, strong minded, logical, focussed, positive and forward thinking goes, I was all of those things and more, but through my own stubborn will to prove to myself and everyone else I was invincible I was brought to near collapse and as close to ending it all as I would ever want to be. This was undoubtedly the darkest time of my life and to this day it will always be a constant reminder of what might have been if it were not for the professionals around me at that time. Eighteen months later, I am still on the tablets and will be for the foreseeable, but the days are getting better and I do at least now see a glimmer of hope; something I once didn't think I would ever see again. I am glad my family never knew just how bad things had got with me and I know that I had shut them out for such a long time locked away in my own little bubble, hibernating in my past. Had I not had the specialist help from Dr Harper, I doubt very much I would be here today.

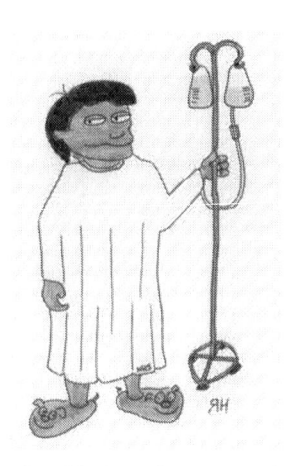

42. Grinding Halt

Commitment and dedication is all about not giving in, and goodness knows I have had plenty of things thrown at me in the last couple of years. I was starting to make good progress with my breakdown and could actually begin to count good days now and then. I had just finished a viewing at my Cheltenham branch and got home some forty five minutes later at around 9.00 p.m. No soon as I had sat down, I looked over to my wife and said *'I think something is wrong – I don't feel right'*. As I lent forward, the next thing I knew I was bent double and collapsed to the floor in excruciating pain. An ambulance was called immediately and I was rushed off to hospital.

I was immediately admitted into the triage bays where I was injected with morphine to ease the abdominal pain. How anyone can possibly like that stuff is beyond me. As quick as it enters your bloodstream you feel utterly helpless and the sinking feeling that leaves you numb and out of control is quite scary as you feel as if you are falling through the bed with the sheets and bed pillows enveloping you like a noose. Your muscles and limbs become heavy as if hypnotised and you feel the shallowness of breath slow down to an almost flat line level, yet strangely a feeling of euphoria and an outer body sensation of warmth takes over. The pain was still present when I was asked if I wanted more. I didn't care; I just wanted the pain to go away. A minute can seem like a lifetime when you are in agony and I was in no way exaggerating the extreme pain that I was going through.

The Doctors were able to diagnose the symptons quickly and accurately and I was admitted into one of the tower block wards for observation and treatment. With no history or hint of warning I had collapsed with kidney stones and until they passed I was there to stay on a prescription of morphine and fluids. The plus side to morphine is that it is a very effective way of pain control but the down side is that the nausea brought about violent spasms of sickness, which seemed to trigger off a frog chorus of kidney bowl vomiting from the five other male patients in the bay I shared.

Between sickness and feeling like I had been turned inside out, I was still trying to run a business and from my hospital bed was continuing to make the calls I needed to do to tie up funeral arrangements I had started before I was ill.

By the end of the second day, and still in a lot of pain I was surprised to get a visit by my good friend Andy who is also a Funeral Director. He asked if there was anything he could do, and I said quite stupidly *'well, you could get me out of here for a few hours while I tie up a funeral arrangement'*. *'Are you sure?'* he said, *'I'm sure'* quite determined that I wouldn't let the family down. I phoned ahead to say I would be with them within the hour. Getting out wasn't exactly difficult, I mean it's not like it's a prison even if I did feel as if I had broken out. Andy drove me home as I needed to get a change of clothes before I popped out to see the family. I still had the cannula in situ which obviously had to be removed before I went anywhere. Andy said to me with a cunning smile *'quick or slow?'* I didn't get the chance to give him an answer one way or the other when I felt a quick tug as the tube ripped away from my hand. No soon as it was out that the back of my hand started to balloon the size of a golf ball, I guess from the way that the cannula had been yanked out.

While getting dressed in my work gear the telephone rang and it was the hospital to ask if I had been seen as I was not on the wards. Andy had said I had just popped home to pick up a couple of things. They were not best pleased and said that I should have told someone before taking it upon myself to disappear. The nurse went on to ask if the cannula was still in situ and that I would need to go back and have it removed by trained staff as you are not supposed to just take them out! Well, I suppose that explained why my hand was now the size of half of a tennis ball.

No soon as I got to the family's house to go through the arrangements that I was starting to get nauseous again and I could feel a hot flush coming on. Somehow I managed to get through the arrangement before making my apologies for cutting short the visit as I wasn't feeling too good. I knew the family quite well from a previous family funeral I had helped them with and they were more than understanding and even offered to help carry my case to the car.

As I got back into my car, I knew I had made a grave error by leaving the hospital and was now suffering for the consequences. I don't really remember driving back home; it all seemed a bit of a haze. I just remember being readmitted back into the ward from whence I came, this time with little sympathy from the doctors and nursing staff. I knew my actions were plain right stupid, but when I explained the situation they all agreed that although I had acted irresponsibly they also admired my dedication and unselfishness to helping others.

What I did was wrong, but what else was I suppose to do?

43. Arrangements

Never work with children or animals, well certainly not the latter anyway. Animals are absolutely adorable when they are quiet and fast asleep but when they're not anything goes and sometimes you have to just ignore them.

I remember quite vividly a time when I was sat going through the funeral arrangements with a family when the amorous Jack Russell couldn't contain his urges any longer and decided to start humping my leg. The owner of the dog apologised profusely as I told them not to worry as I wasn't offended. Of course I was offended, but under the circumstances I could hardly send the dog into orbit much as I would have wanted to.

I also remember a time when I was sat in with another family with my back to the wall. I had completely finished all that I needed to go through before easing off the formal side to chat about everyday things. I had noticed pictures of snakes and tarantulas on the wall and thought it a bit strange when most people tend to have portraits or landscapes.

I asked about the unusual choice of decor to which they said quite simply that they kept snakes and spiders in the house. All of a sudden I started to feel a little uneasy as I can honestly say I am not a lover of anything that has more than four legs.

Slightly uncomfortable by this I asked, not really wanting to know the answer *'where do you keep them then?'*

''you've been sat next to them for the last hour' was the reply. Trying not to show that it bothered me I thanked them for the cup of tea and left.

Recently on another occasion, I was greeted by a lady who owned a chameleon and a water dragon. The chameleon as expected was amazingly camouflaged against the patterned curtain perched high on the curtain rail looking down, observing every movement I made. *'don't worry about him'* the lady said *'he'll be alright if I put a DVD of Queen on – for some reason he loves their music and won't trouble us while it's playing'*. Now I have been fairly naive over the years and have been caught out a few times and knew this must have been another wind up. To my surprise it wasn't. Freddie Mercury started singing and the chameleon danced robotically along the curtain pole. I would never have believed it unless I had seen it with my own eyes.

As I made myself comfortable on the leather settee, she then told me about her water dragon, *'Where?'* I said. *'There'* was her reply *'on his pole right beside you'*. The water dragon was a bright green lizard about 8 inches in length. As far as lizards go, I would say that it was also quite pretty. She did tell me that it did jump and was quite mischievous. At this I slid ever so slightly to the right, hopefully out of distance should it decide to make a leap. *'Don't worry, he won't hurt you'*. That was of little relief to me as I didn't fancy the thought of some reptiles claws dug into my neck.

Just as I was coming to a close and about to pack up my case I heard a thud on the laminate flooring below. I looked over to see the water dragon flat on his back. *'The silly old sod'* she said *he's always doing that'*. Genuinely concerned I asked if he was alright. *'He'll be fine, he's forever missing the arm of the chair and bouncing off backwards'*.

Thank goodness for leather settees I say.

44. R's

One of my all time favourite films is the life of Brian. I never understood the film as a child but the more I listened to the soundtrack on the CD in my car the more I began to understand the parody. A particular scene that always sticks in my mind is the one where Pilate (who cannot pronounce his R's) addwesses the peoples of Jewusalem to welease a wongdoer from their pwisons.

I remember only too well of a lady who had passed away in a nursing home that had no family to speak of save the nursing staff that had cared for her for the last eight years of her life. On the day of the cremation there was as expected just a handful of nursing staff from the home to see Robbie on her way.

Reverend Roger Roberts presiding suffered the same speech impediment as Monty Python's Pilate. The vicar led the bearers into the chapel reading the opening sentences.

'I am the wessurection and the life says the Lowd...' the chuckles from the nursing staff already start. As I direct

everyone to their seats the vicar continues ' *we bwought nothing into the wold, and we take nothing out. The Lowd gave, and the Lowd has taken away; blessed be the name of the Lowd.*

On his introduction he carries on, *'we meet in the name of Jesus Chwist, who died and was waised to the glowy of God the Father. Gwace and mercy be with you'. 'We have come here today to wemember befowe God our sister Wobbie; to give thanks for her life; to commend her body to God our merciful wedeemer and judge; to commit her body to be cwemated and to comfowt one another in our gwief.*

The hymn is announced:

'Please wemain standing as we sing together the old wugged cross'

At this point, you just knew that the next 20 minutes was not going to get less bearable. I at least had the advantage of choosing my pew at the back of the chapel so as not to be influenced by the antics of the nursing staff that were now in full swing of singing the old rugged cross.

Predictably the rest of what followed was equally painful. At one point I could see one of the care assistants with tears rolling down her face; I have a feeling though it may have been through trying not to laugh. The rest of the nursing staff also tried their level best to hold it together as the vicar constantly referred to Robbie as Wobbie. The committal came not a moment too soon and ended:

'We have entwusted our sister Wobbie to God's mercy, and we now commit her body to be cwemated: earth to earth, ashes to ashes, dust to dust in sure and certain hope of the wessurection to eternal life thwough our Lowd Jesus Chwist, who will twansform our fwail bodies that they may be confowmed to his glowious body, who died was buwied, and wose again fow us. To him be the glowy fow eva and eva. Amen'.

Closing thought: Amen!

45. Conclusion

When asked the question – Was it worth it? You would think it might deserve a quick and positive answer.

My answer is:

If you can afford to put your life on hold for the term you set yourself, I would say, yes.

If you are prepared to work unreservedly 24/7 for as long as it takes, I would say yes.

If you are prepared to sacrifice whatever social life you had for the sake of your goal, I would say yes.

If you are prepared to put the business before everything including family, I would say yes.

If you are so driven and focussed that no matter what it takes to succeed, I would say yes.

If you are strong enough mentally and physically never to give in to illness even if your legs were hanging off, I would still say yes.

I did all of the above without hesitation and paid the price in more ways than I can ever count.

If you have to think about any of the above for just one moment then you should already know what the answer is.

In hindsight my choices would have been very different.

When I started out on this venture my motives went completed against the grain of my advisors who in their respective roles compared success to money. Through sheer grit and determination I did succeed, but it was never about the financial recompense. I had set out to be successful in a different way. I needed to prove to myself that I could own and run my own Funeral Directors.

I had money once but it turned me into someone I didn't like very much and the materialism it brought was nothing more than a fascia. Short of winning the lottery I still have no great fortune and in any case even if I did – no amount of money ever compensates your physical or mental well being.

At one of my low points someone once reminded me *'you came from a council estate and you'll end up back in one'*. That part was true, I did, but it was said as if it were demining that that should be a bad thing. That low point just so happened to be the pivotal juncture and base to what I have become today. Odd that I should be grateful for what at the time seemed to be a useless situation.

Mr Compton had asked me where I saw myself in 20 years time. I said nonchalantly; *'One day I will own my own Funeral Directors'*. At 16, I realised just how stupid that would have sounded.

Now looking back over the last 30 years I would say, be careful what you wish for, one day it might come true.

Printed in Great Britain
by Amazon